FOOD FOR FRIENDS

Cooked.

FOOD FOR FRIENDS

Edited by Ariana Klepac

hardie grant books

CONTENTS

HIGH TEA

SUNDAY ROAST

ULTIMATE PICNIC

DRINKS PARTY CANAPÉS

FOOD FOR FRIENDS

Cooked.com brings Hardie Grant's and Quadrille's ever-growing library of food books into one digital space, and is now home to 23,000 recipes from leading chefs and cooks.

One of life's great pleasures is sharing food with family and friends. At Cooked we believe that every meal can be sensational, so we've brought together top chefs and cooks from around the world to inspire you every day.

Cooked.com is now home to 23,000 tried and tested recipes from leading chefs and cooks. You'll find culinary inspiration from creative Australian chefs Paul Wilson, Luke Nguyen, Mark Best and Ben O'Donoghue; fail-safe classics from Margaret Fulton, Gabriel Gaté, Lyndey Milan and Charmaine Solomon; plus Michelin-star-studded recipes from Alain Ducasse, Mark Hix and, the godfather of pasta, Antonio Carluccio.

Our online recipe collection is constantly expanding, with new books from celebrated authors added all the time. A Cooked membership grants you unlimited access to this virtual library, with 180 gorgeous titles waiting to be devoured. And we wanted to share some of that magic with you.

In this book you'll find 100 handpicked recipes for stress-free entertaining, taking you from languid weekend brunches to spontaneous dinner parties, which are sure to impress your guests. Whip up an indulgent high tea of cakes, pastries and savoury tarts. Fire up the grill for a laid-back barbecue with a Latin accent. Or linger over a sumptuous Sunday roast with all the trimmings. Vegetarians will love our virtuous plant-based feast. Picnics get a modern makeover with imaginative salads, Greek cheese pies and Javanese meatballs. And your next drinks party will be a roaring success with our menu of moreish canapés.

There's something in here to suit every time frame and budget, from super-quick and easy ideas to more challenging showstoppers.

For more fabulous recipes from our family of talented foodies, visit Cooked.com.

Happy cooking,

Sarah Gamboni
Editor, *Cooked*

Tuscan chestnut savoury pancakes (page 146). Photographer Chris Middleton

WEEKEND BRUNCH

Chris Middleton

Next time you plan a weekend get-together with friends, don't discount brunch. Whether served indoors or out, in summer or winter, the recipes here cover all bases — from Mark Hix's wild garlic and cheese bread to Lyndey Milan's apple and blackberry muffins, or Paul Wilson's Mex-inspired French toast with sweetcorn, pancetta and avocado.

Bacon fans will enjoy Fern Green's maple-glaze (she warns it's addictive), paired here with turkey patties and eggs. Alternatively, Greg and Lucy Malouf's white zucchini omelette is a meat-free favourite.

There are drinks in the offing, too: a luscious hot chocolate recipe by Fern Green, using grated dark and milk chocolate (and cream!), and Kate Bradley's vegan chai, made with coconut cream and soy milk.

WHITE ZUCCHINI OMELETTE
WITH MINT AND MELTING CHEESE

Greg and Lucy Malouf, *New Feast*

We learnt to make *kuku-ye sabzi*, one of Persia's best-loved omelettes, during our travels around Iran. It is similar in texture to a frittata, thick with herbs and leafy green vegetables (*sabzi* means 'greenery' in farsi), and sometimes comes garnished with walnuts or barberries. We love to add grated zucchini – especially white zucchini, which are more delicate and less bitter than the dark green variety – although either will do. Cheese is a deviation from the purist Iranian *kuku* but, hot from the oven, its melting softness is irresistible. Try to find a cumin-flavoured gouda if you can. A non-stick, ovenproof frying pan – no more than 20 cm diameter – is ideal for making *kuku*. We've also made this very successfully in a non-stick cake tin.

SERVES 4

—

100 ml olive oil
1 onion, finely diced
1 teaspoon freshly grated
    nutmeg
1 teaspoon dried mint
350 g white zucchini (*about 3*),
    coarsely grated
4 eggs
2 tablespoons self-raising flour
grated zest of 1 lemon
½ teaspoon salt
½ teaspoon freshly ground
    black pepper
200 g gouda (*preferably cumin-
    flavoured, or any other melting
    cheese*), grated
Greek-style yoghurt to serve
    (*optional*)
rosemary for garnish (*optional*)

Preheat the oven to 180°C. Heat half the oil in a frying pan over low heat and fry the onion until it softens. Stir in the nutmeg and mint and fry for another minute. Remove from the heat and leave to cool.

Pour the remaining oil into a non-stick, ovenproof frying pan and heat it in the oven for 5–10 minutes.

Squeeze the grated zucchini firmly to remove as much moisture as possible. Whisk the eggs in a large bowl until frothy. Whisk in the flour, lemon zest, salt and pepper, followed by the zucchini, onion mixture and cheese. The mixture will be quite sloppy.

Pour the mixture into the hot oil. Cover the pan with a lid or some foil and bake in the oven for 10 minutes or until nearly set. Remove the lid and cook for a further 10 minutes to brown the surface.

Cut into wedges and serve hot from the pan with Greek-style yoghurt, if desired. Alternatively, drain on paper towel and cut into wedges when cold to serve with pickles or relish as desired. Garnish with rosemary, if desired.

SPANISH BAKED EGGS

Brent Owens, *Dig In!*

I'm a big fan of Spanish food, especially the smoky paprika and chorizo, and this is one of my favourite breakfasts. Remember that the capers and anchovies are very salty, so taste, taste, taste throughout cooking to check the seasoning. If you're in a hurry, you can put your baking dishes in the oven at preheating stage to warm them up. This will speed up the cooking of the eggs, but remember the dishes will be smoking hot!

SERVES 2
—

250 g chorizo, sliced
2 French shallots, thinly sliced
1 garlic clove, finely chopped
¼ teaspoon smoked paprika
¼ teaspoon ground cumin
¼ teaspoon cayenne pepper
2 tablespoons sherry vinegar
    or red wine vinegar
400 g tinned diced tomatoes
1 teaspoon baby capers, rinsed
    (optional)
2 anchovy fillets, chopped
    (optional)
2 eggs, at room temperature
chopped flat-leaf parsley
    for garnish
chargrilled or toasted bread
    to serve

Preheat the oven to 190°C. Cook the chorizo in a small ovenproof frying pan over medium heat until the oil is released and the chorizo is caramelised, about 2–3 minutes. Add the shallots and garlic and sauté for a further 2 minutes. Add the paprika, cumin and cayenne pepper and sauté for a further minute or until fragrant.

Add the vinegar and deglaze the pan, cooking until the liquid has almost evaporated, about 2 minutes. Add the tomatoes, capers (if using) and anchovies (if using), stir well to combine and continue to cook for another minute.

If you want to serve the eggs in individual dishes, transfer the mixture to two 300 ml ovenproof dishes, otherwise you can just leave the mixture in the frying pan. Make a small indentation in the mixture in the pan or each dish, and break an egg into it. Bake in the oven for 8–10 minutes, depending on how runny you want your yolk. Top with some freshly chopped parsley before serving with the chargrilled or toasted bread.

Mark Roper

OAT, RICOTTA AND BERRY PANCAKES WITH THYME HONEY

Molly Brown, *Grains*

These are so light it's hard to believe they contain oats. Change the berries according to what's in season – blackberries and blackcurrants are good too.

SERVES 4
—
250 g fresh ricotta

3 eggs, 1 whole and 2 separated

50 g wholemeal flour

50 g soft light brown sugar

25 g rolled oats

25 g unsalted butter, melted and cooled, plus non-melted butter for frying

finely grated zest of 1 lemon

125 g blueberries or raspberries icing sugar, sifted, for dusting

thyme honey or any floral honey

Drain the ricotta and mash it with the whole egg and the two yolks. Add the flour, brown sugar, oats, melted butter and lemon zest. Gently stir in the berries, mixing carefully so they don't break up too much. Beat the two egg whites until stiff and then fold them into the mixture.

Melt a knob of butter in a non-stick frying pan over medium heat and spoon enough of the batter in to make a pancake the size of your palm. If you are using a fairly big pan you should be able to cook about three pancakes at the same time.

Cook the pancakes until set underneath and stable enough to turn. Flip the pancakes and cook until golden and set in the middle. The pancakes should take 3–4 minutes on the first side and 2 minutes on the other. As they cook, remove them from the pan and keep them warm in a 150°C oven in a single layer or between sheets of baking paper. Add more butter to the pan as needed but be careful not to burn it. Serve the pancakes dusted with icing sugar and drizzled with honey.

TURKEY PATTIES
WITH MAPLE BACON

Fern Green, *Breakfast: Morning, Noon and Night*

These pair up well with any type of eggs you fancy, from scrambled to boiled. Maple bacon can turn into an addiction. Remember – you have been warned.

SERVES 4

—

2 slices stale white bread
450 g minced turkey
1 garlic clove, grated
1 egg
4 spring onions, thinly sliced
2 tablespoons parsley,
    finely chopped
1½ teaspoons salt
½ teaspoon freshly ground
    black pepper
oil for frying
8 rashers streaky bacon
2 tablespoons maple syrup
4 eggs, extra, cooked in any
    style, to serve

Preheat the oven to 200°C. For the patties, soak the bread in a bowl of cold water for 1 minute, then squeeze out the water and crumble the bread into a large bowl. Add the minced turkey, garlic, egg, spring onion, parsley and seasoning, and combine everything together. With wet hands, shape the mixture into eight golf ball-sized balls and flatten them into patties using the palm of your hand.

Add enough oil to a large frying pan to shallow-fry the patties. Heat the oil and then fry the patties – in batches if necessary – for about 4–5 minutes on each side until they are cooked through and golden brown all over.

While the patties are frying, prepare the bacon. Line a baking tray with baking paper and place the bacon on the paper. Bake for about 15 minutes or until crispy and just beginning to brown.

Keep an eye on the patties as the bacon cooks and, when the patties are done, remove them from the pan and set aside to drain on some paper towel.

Take the bacon out of the oven and, using a pastry brush, coat the bacon with the maple syrup. Put the bacon back in the oven for 3–5 minutes until it has browned and is sticky.

Meanwhile, cook the eggs in your preferred style – you may have to remove the bacon from the oven and set it to one side with the patties for a few minutes while you finish cooking your eggs.

Serve the turkey patties and maple bacon with the eggs.

—

250 ml milk
70 g unsalted butter
1 tablespoon extra-virgin olive oil
125 g plain flour, sifted
finely grated zest of 2 lemons
3 eggs
1 tablespoon honey
1 teaspoon orange blossom water
750 ml vegetable oil

CINNAMON SUGAR

—

1 teaspoon ground cinnamon
150 g caster sugar

HOT LEMON FRITTERS WITH CINNAMON SUGAR

Greg and Lucy Malouf, *Moorish*

These Spanish-inspired fritters are delicious on their own, drizzled with maple syrup, or topped with a blob of whipped cream. They make a fine dessert as well as being ideal pancakes for a lazy weekend brunch.

For the fritters, put the milk, butter and olive oil in a saucepan and heat gently until the butter has completely melted. As soon as the liquid froths up, quickly tip in the flour and lemon zest, and beat well with a wooden spoon to incorporate into the liquid. Continue cooking over low heat for a further 3–4 minutes, beating constantly, until the mixture is glossy and comes away from the sides of the pan in a smooth ball.

Take the pan off the heat and add the eggs, one at a time, while beating the mixture well. Finally, add the honey and orange blossom water. You will end up with a shiny, smooth dough-like batter. Refrigerate the mixture for 2–3 hours, allowing it to stiffen and thicken.

For the cinnamon sugar, combine the ingredients in a shallow dish.

Heat the oil in a deep saucepan (or deep-fryer) to 180°C.

Carefully place teaspoon-sized blobs of the batter into the oil, and cook until golden brown and starting to split – this should only take a couple of minutes.

Remove the fritters from the oil and drain on paper towel, then roll them in the cinnamon sugar mixture. Eat immediately.

SERVES 4

—

900 ml full-cream milk
150 g dark chocolate, grated
    (minimum 70% cocoa)
60 g milk chocolate, grated
150 ml pouring cream
pinch of ground cinnamon
pinch of salt

REALLY CHOCOLATEY HOT CHOCOLATE

Fern Green, *Breakfast: Morning, Noon and Night*

Cold winter mornings equal woolly socks, polo necks and croissants dipped in hot chocolate. I like my hot chocolate dipped into. It reminds me of being in France, copying my French exchange friend; not really knowing how to do it at first and feeling a bit naughty, and very happy with discovering a new way of enjoying hot chocolate. This recipe is über-chocolatey, with a hint of cinnamon just to make it feel a little warmer in the mouth.

To a large saucepan, add 300 ml of the milk and put it over medium heat. Once the milk is warm, stir in both chocolates. When these have melted, whisk in the rest of the milk and the cream. Bring the mixture back up to warm, but not boiling, and add the cinnamon and the salt. Serve in four large mugs.

Danielle Wood

APPLE ᴀɴᴅ BLACKBERRY CRUMBLE MUFFINS

Lyndey Milan, *Lyndey Milan's Taste of Australia*

Logan Brae is a wonderful old apple orchard at Blackheath, the last one in the Blue Mountains. The lovely cook there, Julia, shared her muffin recipe with me.

MAKES 8

—

225 g plain flour
165 g sugar
½ teaspoon salt
2 teaspoons baking powder
80 ml milk
80 ml vegetable oil
1 egg
1 large granny smith apple
115 g blackberries

CRUMBLE

—

75 g plain flour
60 g butter, chilled and cut
    into 1 cm dice
2 tablespoons caster or
    brown sugar
2 tablespoons slivered almonds,
    roughly chopped

Preheat the oven to 180°C. Line eight 125 ml holes of a muffin tin with paper liners or use disposable baking cups.

For the crumble, place the flour in a small bowl. Add the butter and rub it in, using your fingertips, until the mixture resembles breadcrumbs. Stir through the sugar and almonds.

For the muffin mix, combine the flour, sugar, salt and baking powder in a large bowl.

In a small bowl or jug, whisk the milk, oil and egg until smooth.

Peel and core the apple. Cut half into 1 cm dice and grate the remainder.

Add the milk mixture to the dry ingredients with the grated apple, apple dice and blackberries. Mix until just combined. Spoon into the prepared muffin tin or disposable baking cups, sprinkle with the crumble and bake for 25 minutes or until cooked when tested with a skewer.

SWEETCORN FRENCH TOAST
WITH PANCETTA AND AVOCADO

Paul Wilson, *Cantina*

Mexican food is considered one of the world's first fusion cuisines. This traditional corn cake recipe is normally served cold and here has been adapted so it can be sliced and grilled before topping with crispy bacon, avocado and salsa mexicana. It's French toast Mexican style! Maple or agave syrup can be included in this recipe with fresh bananas, if you have a sweet tooth.

SERVES 4

—

100 g thinly sliced pancetta
4 wedges of iceberg lettuce
    or rocket leaves to serve
1 avocado, thickly sliced
micro leaves to serve (*optional*)
1 small red capsicum, thinly
    sliced in rings, to garnish

SWEETCORN LOAF

—

125 g butter
300 g fresh or frozen corn
    kernels (*about 2 corn cobs*),
    plus extra cooked shards
    for garnish (*optional*)
375 g tin condensed milk
60 g sour cream
5 large organic eggs
50 g masa harina PAN flour
1½ teaspoons baking powder
pinch of sea salt
oil for spraying

Preheat the oven to 150°C and lightly grease and line a loaf tin with baking paper.

For the sweetcorn loaf, melt the butter in a large frying pan over low heat. Add the fresh or frozen corn kernels, cover and cook for 5 minutes, or until softened. Add the condensed milk and sour cream and bring to the boil. Reduce the heat and simmer, stirring constantly, for 5 minutes.

Transfer the ingredients to a food processor and blend to make a smooth sauce. Gradually add the eggs, masa harina PAN flour and baking powder, processing on low speed to combine. Season with the sea salt.

Pour the batter into the prepared tin and bake for about 30–40 minutes, until golden brown and a skewer comes out clean when tested. Leave in the tin for 10 minutes to cool slightly, then invert the sweetcorn loaf onto a wire rack to cool completely. Wrap in plastic wrap and refrigerate for at least 4 hours, or preferably overnight.

If you want to make the zesty lime dressing for the salsa mexicana (instead of just using lime juice), combine the lime zest, 100 ml of the lime juice and the sugar in a small saucepan and simmer for 5 minutes, or until the zest is soft. Transfer to a food processor or blender and process, gradually adding the olive oil and remaining juice, until emulsified. Season with the salt. (You can store this in an airtight container in the refrigerator for up to 1 month.)

For the salsa mexicana, combine the onion, tomato, jicama, jalapeño, habanero and coriander in a medium bowl. Just before serving add 150 ml of the zesty lime dressing or lime juice and toss to combine. Season with sea salt.

ZESTY LIME DRESSING

—

finely grated zest of 3 limes
300 ml lime juice
115 g caster sugar
325 ml extra-virgin olive oil
2 teaspoons sea salt

SALSA MEXICANA

—

1 red onion, finely diced
6 cherry tomatoes, quartered
150 g jicama (*or breakfast radish
    or daikon*), finely diced
2 jalapeños, seeded and
    thinly sliced
1 habanero chilli, seeded and
    thinly sliced
4 large handfuls of coriander
    leaves, roughly chopped
150 ml Zesty lime dressing
    (*see above*) or lime juice
sea salt to taste

JALAPEÑO AND FINGER
LIME CREMA

—

250 g sour cream
100 g salted ricotta,
    finely grated
2 green jalapeños, seeded
    and roughly chopped
finely grated zest and juice
    of 3 limes
1 garlic clove, grated
pinch of ground cumin
1 large handful of oregano
    leaves, finely chopped
50 g finger lime flesh or the
    zest and juice of 1 lime
sea salt to taste

For the jalapeño and finger lime crema, combine the sour cream, salted ricotta, jalapeño, lime zest and juice, garlic and cumin in a bowl, and stir to make a smooth cream. Stir in the oregano and finger lime flesh. Season with sea salt. (You can store this in an airtight container in the refrigerator for up to 1 week.)

Preheat an overhead grill to high.

Slice the sweetcorn loaf into eight slices, 2–3 cm thick.

Arrange the pancetta slices on a baking tray and grill them until crisp. Drain off any excess fat and keep warm.

Heat a non-stick frying pan over medium heat. Spray the pan with cooking oil and cook the sweetcorn loaf slices for 2 minutes on each side or until golden brown.

To serve, arrange two pieces of sweetcorn bread on each plate, top with an iceberg wedge and some pancetta and avocado slices. Spoon on some salsa mexicana and a dollop of the crema and garnish with the micro leaves (if using), capsicum and the shards of corn (if using).

See photograph page 24.

NOTES

—

agave syrup Also known as honey water, this sweet syrup is extracted from the same succulent plant that mescal and tequila come from, which grows in the southwestern United States, Mexico and Central America. It is available from supermarkets, gourmet suppliers and Mexican grocery stores.

finger lime The finger lime is a gourmet bush food native to Australia and is sometimes known as lime caviar due to its caviar-like flesh. It has a citrus flavour similar to lime. Available from bush food specialists and some gourmet grocery stores.

jicama Sometimes called the 'Mexican potato', this tuber has crispy white flesh with a nutty flavour, somewhat like a water chestnut. It can be eaten raw or cooked. It is available from some supermarkets and gourmet greengrocers.

masa harina PAN flour Masa harina is a finely ground flour made from hominy (nixtamalised corn). It is used for making masa dough. Also known as harina PAN, this is a type of masa harina flour from Venezuela. It is available from South American grocery stores.

WILD GARLIC AND CHEESE BREAD

Mark Hix, *Mark Hix on Baking*

Wild garlic is a wonderful vegetable to forage for, though you might get stuck on what to do with a large harvest. The combination here of cheese and mellow-flavoured wild garlic is great, with the bread making a perfect light meal, snack or accompaniment to a meal. If you haven't got access to wild garlic then garlic chives will do the job.

MAKES 1–2

—

500 g strong white bread flour, plus extra for dusting

7 g fast-action yeast, mixed with about 150 ml warm water

1 tablespoon clear honey

100 ml olive oil

200 g wild garlic leaves or 200 g garlic chives

2 teaspoons salt

150–200 g mature cheddar, grated

Mix the flour, yeast and honey in a stand mixer fitted with the dough hook for about 2–3 minutes to make a stiff, elastic dough, adding a little more water during mixing to bring the ingredients together, if necessary. Cover the bowl with plastic wrap and leave to prove in a warm place for a few hours until the dough has doubled in volume.

Meanwhile, heat 20 ml of the oil in a frying pan, add the wild garlic leaves and salt and cook until wilted but not coloured. You may need to do this in batches. Leave to cool.

Remove the dough from the bowl and knead it back to its original size on a lightly floured work surface, incorporating the remaining olive oil as you go.

Divide the dough in half for 2 small loaves or leave whole for one large loaf – it's up to you. Shape your dough into 1 or 2 rough rectangles and scatter over the wild garlic and three-quarters of the cheese. Roll the dough up tightly widthways and transfer, seam side down, to a lightly oiled baking tray. Cover with a damp tea towel and leave to prove until doubled in size.

Preheat the oven to 240°C. Score the top of your bread a few times then dust lightly with flour. Scatter the remaining cheese down the centre. Bake in the oven for 15 minutes. Turn the oven down to 200°C and bake for a further 15–20 minutes. Remove from the oven and leave to cool.

LEFT
Sweetcorn French toast with pancetta and avocado (recipe page 22)

HOMEMADE VEGAN CHAI

Kate Bradley, *Kenko Kitchen*

I am a huge chai enthusiast. It makes me feel relaxed and at ease. The spices warm my belly and it's so pleasurable to consume. I love chai hot or cold, so here are two ways to have my favourite spiced tea.

SERVES 4

CHAI SPICE

—

60 ml black tea
3 cinnamon sticks
6 star anise
6 cardamom pods
8 cloves
½ teaspoon freshly
    grated nutmeg
¼ teaspoon ground ginger
1½ tablespoons cacao powder
seeds from 1 vanilla bean
50 g coconut sugar or rice
    malt syrup

CREAMER MILK

—

500 ml coconut cream
500 ml soy milk

For iced chai, begin by mixing all the chai spice ingredients together with 500 ml water in a saucepan. Bring to the boil over medium heat and then reduce the heat to low and let simmer for 15 minutes (up to 30 minutes if you want a stronger chai taste). Remove from the heat, strain and place the liquid in a bottle.

For the creamer milk, mix the coconut cream and soy milk together.

Pour the chai into a glass filled with ice, and top with the desired amount of creamer.

Alternatively, for a warm milk chai, simply omit the water with the chai spice ingredients and use the creamer instead. Warm the chai and milk up in a saucepan for 10 minutes or until the milk has turned a beautiful caramel colour, strain and enjoy.

NOTES

—

cacao powder is the result of pulverising raw cacao beans and separating the powder from the cacao butter. This is the raw version of cocoa and still has all the nutrients of the cacao bean. Use it as a replacement for cocoa for a huge boost of nutrients in your food. Available in supermarkets, health food stores, organic supermarkets and online.

coconut sugar is the evaporated granular form of coconut nectar. It has a low GI and is derived from the coconut palm blossom. It is a good sugar and brown sugar alternative and has a rich caramel-like taste. Available from most supermarkets, grocers and online.

rice malt syrup is a syrup made from brown rice. It is a healthy alternative to sugar and contains zero fructose. It has a honey-like consistency and is great used in cooking or even as a spread. It is gluten-free and contains complex carbohydrates. Available from most supermarkets, health food stores and organic supermarkets.

Elisa Watson

BACKYARD GRILL

We think most things taste better on the barbecue. When you're entertaining outside, the sounds and smells of sizzling, smoking and caramelising add a welcome sense of theatre, too.

The usual suspects are here — from beef and chicken to corn and onions — but with requisite wow factor, including recipes with a Southeast Asian or Latin vibe.

Michele Curtis' barbecued prawns cooked in a teriyaki marinade are sure crowd pleasers, while Ben O'Donoghue's barbecued banana split will look after the sweet tooths. More substantial dishes are Adrian Richardson's barbecued butterflied lamb, or coconut grilled chicken thighs with a lovely sweet chilli sauce from Leanne Kitchen and Antony Suvalko.

Brent Owens' American-style sticky pork ribs are a favourite. They're marinated in Coca-Cola. And yes, they absolutely taste as good as they look.

AMERICAN-STYLE STICKY PORK RIBS

Brent Owens, *Dig In!*

Ribs are 'fingers only' food. They're messy, fun, sticky and damn good. Adding the Coca-Cola gives the ribs a complex molasses sweetness and this intensifies and caramelises when cooked. Yum! This is comfort food, so carry on the vibe and serve with potato wedges with blue cheese sauce or chips.

SERVES 4
—
2 x 375 ml bottles dry cider
125 ml cider vinegar
2 large racks pork ribs

DRY RUB
—
1 tablespoon onion powder
1 tablespoon garlic powder
1 tablespoon cayenne pepper

MARINADE
—
1 x 375 ml can Coca-Cola
125 ml tomato sauce
125 ml dry apera (*sherry*)
55 g brown sugar
3 garlic cloves, crushed
2 tablespoons Tabasco sauce

Preheat the barbecue to high with the hood closed.

For the dry rub, put the onion powder, garlic powder and cayenne pepper in a bowl and stir to combine.

Put the cider, cider vinegar and 500 ml water in a large roasting dish and place a roasting rack on top. Dust the ribs lightly with the dry rub then place them on the roasting rack. Cover tightly with foil and cook on the barbecue, with the hood closed, for 1 hour.

Meanwhile, for the marinade, put all the ingredients in a large saucepan over medium heat and cook for 20 minutes or until thickened, stirring every few minutes.

Remove the ribs from the barbecue and discard the liquid. Brush on a thick layer of the marinade. Place the ribs directly on the barbecue over medium heat and grill to char the outside. Cook until both sides are charred, about 5–10 minutes, brushing with the marinade and turning every few minutes.

Alternatively, you can cook the ribs in a 160°C oven for 1 hour. Transfer the ribs to a roasting tin, increase the oven temperature to 220°C, brush with the marinade and cook for 15-20 minutes, turning the ribs over every 5 minutes.

—

125 ml light soy sauce
2 tablespoons lemon juice
1 tablespoon rice vinegar
2 tablespoons mirin
2 garlic cloves, crushed
1 tablespoon grated ginger
oil
freshly ground black pepper
1 kg raw prawns, peeled
    and deveined
lemon wedges to serve

TERIYAKI BARBECUED PRAWNS

Michele Curtis, *What's for Dinner?*

You can barbecue the prawns as they are, or thread them onto skewers.

Mix together the soy sauce, lemon juice, rice vinegar, mirin, garlic, ginger and 1 tablespoon of oil and season with the pepper. Pour over the prawns and toss to combine.

Preheat the barbecue until hot. Thread the prawns onto skewers, if desired, and brush lightly with oil. Cook for 1–2 minutes on each side, until the flesh turns opaque. Serve straight away with lemon wedges.

MAKES 500 ML

—

1½ tablespoons cumin seeds
2 garlic cloves, crushed
100 ml sherry vinegar
125 ml olive oil
200 ml pomegranate juice
    or molasses
2 tablespoons sugar
40 g sesame seeds, toasted
sea salt and freshly ground
    black pepper

POMEGRANATE MOJO

Paul Wilson, *Cantina*

This is a signature sauce of Latin cooking, said to be the condiment of the Portuguese explorers who left their garlic scent throughout their travels. So many nations have now added their own accents and that's the charm of this popular sauce. The sourness that interplays with the garlic is the key and I choose to add pomegranate for its striking and full zesty zing. This sauce can be used to invigorate barbecued meats, soups or stews or to dress raw sashimi-grade fish.

Place the cumin seeds in a dry frying pan and sprinkle with water to moisten. Cook over low heat until the water evaporates and the seeds begin to dry-fry and become fragrant. Add the garlic and vinegar and cook for 30 seconds. Add 1½ tablespoons of the oil and gently warm over low heat for 2 minutes, or until the garlic is cooked. Transfer to a blender and process, gradually adding the remaining oil, the pomegranate juice or molasses and the sugar. Stir in the sesame seeds. Season with salt and pepper. Store in an airtight container in the refrigerator for up to 1 week.

BALSAMIC ROSEMARY ONIONS

Ben O'Donoghue, *Ben's BBQ Bible*

A barbecue just doesn't feel like a barbecue unless there are onions. This recipe is a great way to serve them as an accompaniment to whole joints of beef or lamb cooked on the barbecue. I like to use a charcoal fire for this one — which isn't to say that cooking the onions over gas won't be as awesome! Make sure the onions you choose have firm, intact and clean skins. The flavours in this recipe are akin to sweet and sour: you have the wonderful sweetness of the slow-cooked onion, and the woody, sweet and sharp flavour of the balsamic. Try cooking them in a conventional oven as well, I would recommend cooking them for 45 minutes at about 160°C.

SERVES 6

—

6 onions
120 ml balsamic vinegar
salt
freshly ground black pepper
300 g butter, cut into 12 cubes
6 rosemary sprigs

Prepare your barbecue for cooking to medium heat.

Cut a deep cross into the top of each onion, cutting one-third of the way into each one.

Force your thumb into the incision of each onion and prise it open a little. Place 1–2 teaspoons of the vinegar inside, then season with salt and pepper. Press a cube of butter into each onion, followed by a sprig of rosemary.

Arrange three squares of foil per onion. Place each onion in the centre of the layers of foil, bring the edges up and together over the top of the onion and twist lightly together.

Place around the edges of your charcoal fire or over the direct heat of a gas grill. Cook for 30–40 minutes, until the onions are tender to the prick of a small sharp knife.

Remove the packages from the fire and carefully untwist the foil. Gently prise open the onions and divide the remaining butter and vinegar among them. Taste with your fingers and correct the seasoning.

Rewrap the onions and allow them to cook for a further 10 minutes.

Once cooked, remove the onions from the heat and allow them to stand for a few minutes. Remove from the foil and transfer to a serving plate.

To serve, gently squeeze the bottom of the onions as you would a baked potato, so they open a little.

BARBECUED SNAPPER
WITH CAPSICUM

Luca Lorusso and Vivienne Polak, *Sharing Puglia*

The Ionian and Adriatic seas meet at the tip of the heel of Puglia in Italy and provide an abundance of fish, including orata, or snapper. All year round the fishermen haul vast loads of fish and sell directly from the ports that dot the coastline. At Mola di Bari on a recent visit, Vivienne and I wandered around the port, which was a hub of activity. There were men in caps smoking, drinking strong coffee, noisily playing cards and discussing 'world politics' (or football, in other words). The fish in this recipe is barbecued. We love barbecuing as it's such a laid-back way to cook and entertain family and friends, and it leaves little mess in the kitchen.

SERVES 6
—

1.5–2 kg whole snapper, cleaned
extra-virgin olive oil for drizzling
2 lemons

PEPERONI
—

60 ml olive oil
1 onion, sliced
2 garlic cloves, peeled
6 assorted capsicums, cut into
    large dice
400 g tinned peeled tomatoes,
    quartered
handful of pitted black olives
2 bay leaves
pinch of sugar
80 ml red wine vinegar, or more
    if necessary
handful of fresh oregano or
    1 teaspoon dried oregano
handful of flat-leaf parsley,
    roughly chopped
salt
freshly ground black pepper

For the peperoni, heat the olive oil in a frying pan over medium heat and sauté the onion and whole garlic cloves until soft. Add the capsicum, tomato, olives, bay leaves, sugar, red wine vinegar and 100 ml water. Cook, covered, for 30 minutes, then add the oregano and parsley. Check the pan and add more water if the capsicum and tomato look too dry. (There should always be some liquid in the pan.) Cook for a further 15 minutes, or until the vegetables have softened but are not mushy.

Season the peperoni well with salt and freshly ground black pepper and allow to cool. Transfer to a jar if you want to store it, or serve at room temperature for up to 1 week.

To prepare the fish, rinse it inside and out and dry with paper towel. Make three diagonal shallow cuts approximately 1 cm deep in the side of the fish and rub generously with olive oil and salt. Cut one of the lemons into rough wedges and place these in the cavity of the fish.

Place a large sheet of foil on a work surface and place a piece of baking paper, the same size as the fish, on top of that.

Preheat a barbecue with a hood to medium. (If you want to cook the fish in the oven, preheat it to 200°C.)

Place the fish on the baking paper and enclose the fish, securing the foil around the fish. Place the fish on the barbecue grill and close the hood. Reduce the heat to low and cook for approximately 20 minutes. Turn the fish over halfway through cooking time.

Check the fish by carefully opening up the parcel and inserting a knife into the flesh. The flesh should be flaky and white. Take the fish parcel off the barbecue and place it on a cool baking tray to rest for a few moments.

Open the parcel and carefully place the fish on a large platter. Cut the remaining lemon into wedges and place around the fish. Drizzle with extra-virgin olive oil and serve with the prepared peperoni. Season with salt and pepper to taste and serve.

Mark Roper

'BLACK ROAST' VENEZUELAN SUGAR-CRUSTED BEEF

Rachael Lane, *South American Grill*

Asado negro is the signature dish of Venezuela's capital, Caracas. It is traditionally slow-roasted in the oven, but has been adapted here to make it suitable for the barbecue. The sugar, vinegar, worcestershire sauce and garlic marinade creates a sweet, yet balanced, black glaze on the meat once cooked, leaving the centre pink and juicy. Plantains are typically used for cooking savoury dishes. They are eaten in parts of South America, Africa and Southeast Asia. They are cooked in similar ways to potatoes and can be steamed, boiled or fried. Here they are coated in breadcrumbs, but they are commonly fried without them. They are traditionally served to accompany grilled meats.

SERVES 8
—

185 g soft brown sugar
250 ml white wine vinegar
60 ml worcestershire sauce
6 garlic cloves, crushed
½ teaspoon freshly ground
    black pepper
2 kg whole scotch fillet
steamed rice to serve *(optional)*

GRILLED PLANTAIN
IN BREADCRUMBS
—

5 large green plantain bananas
4 large eggs
200 g dry breadcrumbs
60 g butter
2 tablespoons vegetable oil

Combine the sugar, vinegar, worcestershire sauce, garlic and pepper in a medium-sized bowl.

Place the scotch fillet in the bowl, coat in the sugar mixture, cover and leave to marinate in the refrigerator for 2–4 hours.

Preheat a gas barbecue with a hood to 180°C. All the burners should be set to medium.

Remove the meat from the refrigerator and allow it to come to room temperature, then transfer the fillet to a large roasting tin and insert a meat thermometer into the centre of the meat. Reserve the marinade. Place the tray in the centre of the barbecue and turn off the burners directly underneath. Cover and cook for 1 hour for medium—rare, basting occasionally with the remaining marinade, or until the meat thermometer reads 55°C.

For the plantains, preheat a gas barbecue grill plate to medium. Cut the plantains in half lengthways.

Lightly beat the eggs in a large shallow bowl. Place the breadcrumbs on a tray. Dip the plantain halves first into the egg and then roll to coat in the breadcrumbs, pressing to coat all over.

Heat the butter and vegetable oil together in a small saucepan, until the butter has melted.

Grease the grill plate with half of the butter mixture. Cook the plantains for 3–5 minutes on one side, drizzle with the remaining butter mixture, then turn and cook the other side for a further 3–5 minutes, until golden brown and soft.

Remove the tray with the meat from the barbecue, cover the meat with foil and set aside to rest for 15 minutes. Cut the scotch fillet into slices and serve with steamed rice (if using) and the plantains.

BARBECUED CHICKEN WINGS
WITH ANNATTO OIL

Tracey Lister and Andreas Pohl, *Vietnamese Street Food*

In Hanoi, the legendary Ly Van Phuc Street, also simply and somewhat unimaginatively known as 'Chicken Street', specialises in this dish. Rows of stalls on each side of the street keep the barbecues burning late into the night, plying hungry revellers with tasty chicken washed down with cheap beer. You can purchase annatto oil from Asian supermarkets, but I've provided a recipe.

SERVES 6

—

12 chicken wings
4 garlic cloves, finely chopped
2 red Asian shallots, finely
    chopped
⅓ teaspoon five-spice powder
1 teaspoon brown sugar
½ teaspoon freshly ground
    black pepper
1 teaspoon annatto oil (*see below*)
1 tablespoon fish sauce
2 teaspoons soy sauce

ANNATTO OIL

—

500 ml canola oil
2 tablespoons annatto seeds

For the annatto oil, put the canola oil and annatto seeds in a saucepan and gently heat for 1 hour, or until the oil takes on a deep red colour. Do not allow the oil to boil or become too hot or it will taste bitter. When the oil is completely cool, strain it through a fine sieve and discard the annatto seeds. (You can store the oil in a sealed jar for up to 4 weeks.)

Separate the chicken wings at the joint so that the chicken cooks evenly.

Prepare the marinade by combining the remaining ingredients.

Place the chicken wings in a baking dish and pour over the marinade. Refrigerate for 1 hour, turning occasionally.

Heat a charcoal grill or barbecue and cook the chicken for 3–4 minutes on each side, until the skin is crisp and char lines appear.

Michael Fountoulakis

ARGENTINIAN GRILLED GARLIC AND ROSEMARY FLATBREAD

Rachael Lane, *South American Grill*

No South American barbecue is complete without bread. These flatbreads (*pan con ajo y romero a la parilla*) have the consistency of pizza dough. They are extremely easy to make and the garlic and rosemary oil infuses a wonderful flavour when the dough is grilled.

SERVES 8

FLATBREAD

—

525 g plain flour
2 teaspoons sea salt
2 teaspoons active dried yeast
1 tablespoon olive oil

GARLIC AND ROSEMARY OIL

—

2 garlic cloves, finely chopped
60 ml extra-virgin olive oil
2 teaspoons sea salt
1 small handful of fresh
    rosemary leaves

For the flatbread, put the flour, salt, yeast, oil and 1⅓ cups warm water in the bowl of a stand mixer fitted with a dough hook. Mix on low–medium speed for 5 minutes, or until the mixture comes together to form a smooth elastic dough. Alternatively, knead the dough by hand for 10–15 minutes. Transfer to a lightly oiled bowl, cover with a clean tea towel and set aside in a warm place to prove for 1–1½ hours, until doubled in size.

Knock back the dough, using your fists to punch out all the air. Shape into four even-sized balls and flatten slightly. Place on lightly oiled baking trays, cover with a clean tea towel and set in a warm place to prove for a further 30 minutes, or until doubled in size.

Preheat a gas or charcoal barbecue to medium–high.

For the garlic and rosemary oil, put all the ingredients in a bowl and stir well to combine.

Flatten the dough out to 1 cm thick discs. Brush the top of each disc with the garlic and rosemary oil and grill, oil side down, for 5 minutes, or until golden brown. Brush the remaining side with the oil, turn and cook for a further 5 minutes, or until cooked through. Cut into wedges and serve the flat bread hot or cold.

—

1 kg boneless pork belly,
   skin removed

1 small garlic bulb, cloves peeled
   and finely chopped

1 onion, finely chopped

55 g soft brown or white sugar

1 teaspoon freshly ground
   black pepper

250 ml soy sauce

125 ml tomato sauce

125 ml lemonade or beer
   (optional)

60 ml calamansi juice or
   lemon juice

20 bamboo skewers, soaked
   in water for 30 minutes

BARBECUED PORK BELLY SKEWERS

Peter Kuruvita, *My Feast*

Cut the pork into long, thin slices, about 5 mm thick and 5 cm wide and place them in a large bowl. Add the remaining ingredients and combine well using your hands. Cover and refrigerate for at least 30 minutes, turning occasionally.

Preheat a charcoal barbecue or regular barbecue grill to medium. Thread the pork strips onto the skewers, reserving the marinade. Barbecue for about 10 minutes until cooked through, turning and basting with the reserved marinade every few minutes.

NOTE

—

Calamansi, calamondin or Philippine lime is a hybrid cumquat of the citrus family. Look for it at specialist greengrocers or farmers' markets.

SERVES 4–6

—

100 g red quinoa, rinsed
   and drained

250 g haloumi, sliced 1 cm thick

juice of 2 lemons

60 ml olive oil

1 bunch mint leaves, finely
   shredded

½ bunch flat-leaf parsley,
   chopped

100 g rocket leaves

PICKLED SHALLOTS

—

60 ml red wine vinegar

2 tablespoons white sugar

2 French shallots, finely diced

HALOUMI AND MINT SALAD WITH PICKLED SHALLOTS

Brent Owens, *Dig In!*

Eat this fresh as the haloumi won't retain its gooey texture once cold. Put a pile of this on barbecued lamb while it's resting to infuse the meat with the delicious flavours.

For the pickled shallots, put the vinegar, 60 ml water and the sugar in a small saucepan over medium heat. Bring to the boil then remove from the heat and add the shallots. Set aside and allow to pickle in the liquid until cool.

Put the quinoa and 250 ml water in a medium saucepan over medium heat. Bring to the boil, then reduce the heat to low and cook, covered, for 12 minutes or until tender. The water will be absorbed. Remove the pan from the heat, remove the lid and allow to sit for 5 minutes. Fluff the quinoa up with a fork and set aside to cool.

Put a chargrill pan over high heat. When hot cook the haloumi for 2 minutes on each side or until golden. Transfer to baking paper and squeeze over the juice of 1 lemon.

Whisk together the remaining lemon juice and the olive oil until well incorporated. Season with salt and pepper. Taste the dressing – it should be very tangy.

Drain the shallots and combine them with the quinoa, herbs and rocket. Drizzle on the dressing then top with the haloumi. Serve immediately.

BARBECUED BUTTERFLIED LAMB
WITH HONEY, ROSEMARY AND TZATZIKI

Adrian Richardson, *Meat*

There are lots of muscles in the leg that all work together as the animal walks and skips around, so it is a really tasty bit of meat with all sorts of different textures to chew on. There is often quite a lot of external fat on the leg that melts in the heat of the barbecue to keep the meat lovely and moist. Be careful not to let it drip onto the charcoal too much, or you'll get flames, which can burn the meat. When you butterfly a leg of lamb – which is a fancy way of saying you remove the bone and open it out flat – it greatly cuts down the cooking time. It also helps the meat absorb all the lovely flavours of the marinade and the barbecue. Sometimes I like to cut the butterflied lamb into pieces and grill them as free-form chunks. If you're not confident about doing the boning and butterflying yourself, ask your butcher to do it for you. This is delicious served with warm pitta bread, tzatziki and maybe a Greek salad. If you are making the tzatziki, you will need to start the day before.

SERVES 6–8
—

1 x 2.5 kg leg of lamb, bone
 removed, butterflied
3 fresh rosemary sprigs, plus
 extra to garnish
125 ml white wine
8 garlic cloves, chopped
60 ml olive oil
60 ml honey
¼ cup parsley, chopped
1 tablespoon salt
1 tablespoon freshly ground
 black pepper
grated zest and juice of 2 lemons
warm pitta bread to serve
 (optional)

TZATZIKI
—

500 g plain yoghurt
1 Lebanese cucumber, peeled
salt
1 garlic clove, crushed
1 tablespoon chopped dill
½ teaspoon ground white pepper
juice of ½ lemon

Open the leg of lamb out flat and trim away any excess fat. Use the tip of a sharp knife to stab grooves into the meat all over. Cut into six even pieces, or leave whole, depending on your mood.

Strip the leaves from the rosemary sprigs and bruise them with a pestle or the flat blade of your knife. Chop roughly and rub them all over the lamb. Transfer to a shallow dish or plastic container that the meat will fit into snugly.

Mix all the remaining ingredients together, except for the lemon zest and juice and pita bread, and pour over the lamb. Use your hands to rub it in well. Cover, refrigerate and leave to marinate overnight or for a few hours.

For the tzatziki, spoon the yoghurt into a clean tea towel or square of muslin. Tie the four corners together and suspend the bundle from a wooden spoon set over a deep bowl. Refrigerate and leave to drain overnight, or for up to 2 days. Split the cucumber in half lengthways, scoop out the seeds and discard them. Grate the cucumber into a small bowl and sprinkle lightly with salt. Leave for 5 minutes then tip into a sieve and rinse. Use your hands to squeeze out as much of the liquid as you possibly can – you want the cucumber to be very dry or it will leak and make your tzatziki watery. Tip the drained yoghurt into a large mixing bowl. Add the cucumber with all the remaining ingredients and stir well. Taste and adjust the seasoning to your liking. (Chill until required, and use within 7 days.)

When ready to cook the lamb, light your barbecue or heat your oven to medium–high. Remove the lamb from the refrigerator and bring it to room temperature. Cook the lamb for around 20–30 minutes for medium–rare, turning continuously. Leave it to rest for 15 minutes in a warm spot before serving. Individual portions will take 10–15 minutes for medium. Just before carving, pour the lemon juice and zest over the lamb. Slice thinly and serve with lots of warm pitta bread (if using), salad of your choice and the tzatziki. Garnish with the extra rosemary sprigs.

COCONUT GRILLED CHICKEN
WITH SWEET CHILLI SAUCE

Leanne Kitchen and Antony Suvalko, *East*

Cooking this chicken might make a slight mess of your barbecue, but it's completely worth it — especially if you cook it as the Thais do, over coals. This is an easy dish that practically everyone loves. If you feel like cooking a Thai feast, it goes perfectly with a Thai-style salad and rice, plus a curry and a simple stir-fry of leafy vegetables. You can cut each thigh in half before marinating, if you are sharing this among a large number of people. Just reduce the cooking time by 6 minutes.

SERVES 6–8 AS PART OF A SHARED MEAL

—

10 chicken thighs on the bone
   (about 2 kg in total)
6 large dried red chillies, soaked
   in boiling water for
   30 minutes, drained
3 lemongrass stems, white part
   only, chopped
2 teaspoons ground coriander
6 garlic cloves, chopped
2 tablespoons chopped fresh
   turmeric or 2 teaspoons
   ground turmeric
300 ml coconut milk
60 ml fish sauce
1 teaspoon ground white pepper
lime wedges to serve

SWEET CHILLI SAUCE

—

75 g medium red chillies,
   chopped
2 garlic cloves, chopped
250 ml white vinegar
1 tablespoon fish sauce
250 g caster sugar

For the sweet chilli sauce, process the chillies and garlic in a food processor until a coarse paste forms. Alternatively, use a mortar and pestle. Transfer to a saucepan, add the vinegar, fish sauce and sugar and bring to a simmer over medium heat, stirring often until the sugar has dissolved. Reduce the heat to low and cook for about 50 minutes, until the mixture has thickened and reduced to a thick pouring consistency. Cool to room temperature. (The sweet chilli sauce will keep, refrigerated, for up to 2 months.)

Using a large, sharp knife, trim the excess bone of each chicken thigh to give a nice shape. Set aside.

Combine the drained chillies in a food processor with the lemongrass, coriander, garlic and turmeric and process until a smooth paste forms. Alternatively, use a mortar and pestle. Combine with the coconut milk, fish sauce and pepper in a large bowl and add the chicken pieces. Using your hands, turn the chicken to coat well in the mixture. Cover the bowl with plastic wrap and refrigerate for 8 hours or overnight.

Remove the chicken from the refrigerator and bring it to room temperature. Drain the chicken well, reserving the marinade and brushing off any solids.

Heat a barbecue or chargrill pan to medium. Add the chicken and cook, turning occasionally and brushing with the reserved marinade from time to time, for about 20 minutes, until the chicken is cooked through. Serve with the sweet chilli sauce and lime wedges.

Leanne Kitchen

Mark Roper

—

100 g walnuts, chopped

1 celeriac

2 granny smith apples

60 ml dry cider

15 g thinly sliced flat-leaf parsley

QUICK WHOLE-EGG PARSLEY MAYO

—

15 g finely chopped flat-leaf
parsley

1 large egg

1 teaspoon dijon mustard

1 tablespoon lemon juice

pinch of salt

250 ml oil (*a blend of 80 ml olive
oil and 170 ml vegetable oil
works well*)

CELERIAC $\overline{\text{AND}}$ APPLE SLAW $\overline{\text{WITH}}$ QUICK WHOLE-EGG PARSLEY MAYO

Brent Owens, *Dig In!*

People don't cook with celeriac that much, but it's soooo good! You can also put this slaw in your tacos or quesadillas or add it to a chicken sandwich.

For the mayo, in a small food processor, pulse the parsley, egg, mustard, lemon juice and salt until combined. With the processor running, add the oil gradually in a slow steady stream, until the mayonnaise is the desired consistency. Check for seasoning. (You can store this in an airtight container in the refrigerator for up to 3 days.) Toast the walnuts in a large dry frying pan over medium–high heat for 4–5 minutes or until fragrant. Set aside to cool.

Chop the celeriac and apples into julienne, or use a mandoline if you have one. Combine with the remaining ingredients, including the mayo, and let sit for 15 minutes to let the flavours infuse and develop before eating.

SERVES 6

—

6 corn cobs, husks removed,
cut in half

125 g mayonnaise

juice of ½ lime

1 tablespoon olive oil

1 teaspoon cayenne pepper

2 teaspoons sweet smoked
paprika

2 teaspoons salt

2 chipotle chillies (*or you can use
2 tablespoons chipotle sauce
or 1–2 teaspoons chipotle
chilli powder – look for these
at gourmet delicatessens, Latin
American supermarkets or
online*)

100 g grated parmesan

lime wedges to serve

MAMASITA CORN ON THE COB

Jane Kennedy, *One Dish. Two Ways*

This recipe is suitable for kids if you omit the cayenne pepper, paprika and chillies.

Bring a large saucepan of water to the boil. Cook the corn for 1 minute, then drain. Combine the mayonnaise and lime juice then divide into two bowls.

Heat the grill of your barbecue or a chargrill pan to a very high heat. Brush the corn with olive oil then cook, turning regularly, for 10–12 minutes, or until charred and tender.

While the corn is grilling, combine the cayenne pepper, paprika and salt in a small bowl.

Heat a small frying pan over high heat then toast the chillies for about 30 seconds on each side, or until fragrant. Remove from the pan and discard the stems and seeds. Coarsely chop the chillies and grind them to a powder using a small food processor or a spice grinder.

Add the chipotle powder or sauce to the lime juice and mayonnaise mixture.

Insert a bamboo cocktail stick into one end of each of the corn pieces. Brush the corn all over with the chipotle mayonnaise. Sprinkle with the paprika mixture and the parmesan and serve with lime wedges.

GRILLED PINEAPPLE WITH RUM, GINGER AND LEMONGRASS SYRUP

Ben O'Donoghue, *Ben's BBQ Bible*

Ben, my pastry chef from the Atlantic Bar and Grill in London, met a Thai girl and travelled to Thailand to meet her family. He came back from his travels inspired by the wonderful food he'd experienced, and was particularly enthused by this recipe for grilled fruit. The really exciting thing about this recipe is the sugar and salt condiment that's served with the fruit. I've come across this spiced sugar before, in David Thompson's kitchen at Nahm in London. The sweet–salty flavours created are so typically Thai. The recipe here is just a guide, as these things are best done according to personal taste. If you prefer more chilli, then add it. With the salt and sugar it's about finding the balance that's right for you, but I would recommend that you err on the side of sweet!

SERVES 4

—

1 pineapple

SYRUP

—

200 ml water
100 ml white rum
100 g sugar
3 cm piece fresh ginger, sliced
1 lemongrass stem, bruised
juice and zest of 1 lemon
juice and zest of 1 lime
1 dried red chilli

SPICED SUGAR

—

1 dried red chilli
2 teaspoons salt flakes
3 teaspoons caster sugar

Remove the skin of the pineapple and cut the flesh into quarters lengthways.

For the syrup, place all the ingredients in a saucepan and bring to the boil, making sure the sugar has dissolved. Remove from the heat and cool, then strain.

Marinate the pineapple in the syrup overnight.

For the spiced sugar, pound the dried chilli and salt, using a mortar and pestle, until you have fine flakes of chilli. Add the caster sugar and stir to combine.

Prepare your barbecue for cooking to medium–high heat. Place the pineapple over the heat and barbecue until caramelised, turning the fruit as required.

Once cooked, skewer the pineapple with bamboo sticks and serve with the spiced sugar as a dipping condiment.

BARBECUED BANANA SPLIT

Ben O'Donoghue, *Ben's BBQ Bible*

Caroline, a good friend of mine, gave me this cracking barbecue recipe. It's nothing revolutionary, but it really appealed to me because I love the combination of bananas and peanut butter. You need a sweet tooth for this one, so don't say I didn't warn you! Be prepared for the kids to start bouncing off the walls. This is a great recipe to make when you're going camping or having a barbecue in the great outdoors as you can prepare the bananas in advance and they travel well.

SERVES 6

—

6 ripe bananas, unpeeled
1 Snickers bar, thinly sliced
1–2 tablespoons runny honey
1–2 tablespoons crushed,
    salted peanuts
cream or ice cream (*vanilla —
    or honeycomb if you're game*),
    to serve

Prepare your barbecue for cooking to medium heat.

Use a sharp knife to make an incision along the length of each banana, being careful not to cut all the way through.

Insert slices of the Snickers bar into the slit bananas, dividing the chocolate equally between the fruit. Drizzle with a little honey, sandwich the bananas back together and wrap in foil.

Place over the direct heat of the barbecue and cook for 5 minutes on each side.

When cooked, unwrap and peel the bananas, sprinkle with the crushed peanuts and serve with cream or ice cream.

HIGH TEA

Who doesn't love the prospect of an afternoon or 'high' tea, with the promise of being spoiled with an array of jewel-like cakes and savoury treats, perhaps served with exotic loose-leaf teas in delicate bone china cups, fresh brewed coffee – or champagne?

You might favour the traditional elegance of Philippa Sibley's rainbow trout rillettes with rye, cucumber and watercress sandwiches, or April Carter's pistachio choux buns. Otherwise, consider Luke Nguyen's knockout tarts with coffee curd and fresh pomegranate, or Tom Hunt's pumpkin doughnut muffins, made from a variation on a doughnut batter, and baked not fried.

Go all out and create a showstopping spread. Or not. Good company and one or two of these recipes alone will do the work of making your guests feel special.

Danielle Wood

RAINBOW TROUT RILLETTES, RYE, CUCUMBER AND WATERCRESS SANDWICHES

Philippa Sibley, *New Classics*

The combinations here are ever so posh. Cucumber and watercress sandwiches with smoked rainbow trout. Perfect after a spot of tennis, lazing on the porch with a nice G and T. Remember these little freshwater trout have delicate flesh and very fine bones. This makes them fiddly but relatively easy to fillet compared to bigger fish — but you can ask your fishmonger to fillet them for you.

SERVES 6

—

1 loaf rye bread (*the best you can find*)
2 small Lebanese cucumbers
100 g soft butter
1 bunch of watercress, leaves, picked and washed

RILLETTES

—

2 x 300 g whole rainbow trout, filleted
100 g unsalted butter, at room temperature
100 g plain yoghurt, at room temperature
1 egg yolk
400 ml freshly squeezed lemon juice
500 ml extra-virgin olive oil
1 x 300 g smoked rainbow trout, skinned and flaked
1 tablespoon chopped chives
1 tablespoon grated fresh horseradish
salt and pepper

For the rillettes, using a razor-sharp knife, make an incision in each fresh rainbow trout from the back of the head to past the front fin. Then, first run the knife down the spine from the head going down towards the tail. Reverse the knife and zip back up towards the head. Cut through the rib cage and remove the fillet.

Because the flesh is so soft and delicate, don't flip the fish over as you would for a more robust beast. Simply make an incision at the tail end and run your knife up the spine, keeping the blade flat and close to the bone and remove the whole skeleton, including the head. Then slide the knife under the rib bones, removing as little flesh as possible.

Pin-bone the fresh trout using fish tweezers, being very careful to remove all bones.

Preheat the oven to 160°C. Place a piece of baking paper on a baking tray. Arrange the four fish fillets skin side down on top. Add a few tablespoons of water and some seasoning. Cover with foil and place in the oven for 4–5 minutes. The fish should be rare at the thickest point. Allow to cool.

Drain off the excess juice. Turn the fillets over and peel off the skin, then remove any dark flesh. Tear the fish into small pieces or flake with a fork.

Put the butter and yoghurt in a mixing bowl and hand-whisk until the mixture becomes fluffy. Alternatively, you can use an electric mixer or food processor. Add the egg yolk and a little of the lemon juice. Drizzle in the extra-virgin olive oil and then add the rest of the lemon juice

Fold through the flaked smoked fish, chives and horseradish. Test for seasoning and add salt and pepper to taste, then set aside.

Slice the rye bread thinly. Thinly slice the cucumbers and season lightly with salt so the cucumber wilts slightly. Butter the bread generously and layer on the cucumber and watercress. Cut the sandwiches into random lengths and serve alongside the rillettes.

Encourage your guests to thickly spread the rillettes onto the sandwiches and eat with their fingers.

Mark Roper

BROWN SUGAR MERINGUES
WITH PASSIONFRUIT CURD

Lyndey Milan, *Lyndey Milan's Taste of Australia*

These meringues are a modern take on an Australian classic – the pavlova with cream and passionfruit. Made as miniatures, they are ideal for afternoon tea or to finish a cocktail party.

MAKES 50

—

3 eggs, separated
80 g caster sugar
80 g brown sugar
1 tablespoon cornflour
1 teaspoon vanilla bean paste
lightly whipped cream to serve

PASSIONFRUIT CURD

—

60 g passionfruit pulp
40 g butter
55 g caster sugar
3 egg yolks (*left over from the meringue mixture*)

Preheat the oven to 160°C and line two baking trays with baking paper.

Using an electric mixer, beat the egg whites until they form stiff peaks. Add the caster sugar then the brown sugar, gradually, and continue to beat until the mixture is glossy and the sugar has dissolved. Add the cornflour and vanilla and mix until just combined.

Spoon or pipe the meringue onto the prepared trays. With the back of a wet teaspoon, carefully make an indent in each meringue that will hold the cream and curd. Bake for 50 minutes or until dry. Place the trays on wire racks and leave to cool. Carefully peel the meringues off the baking paper.

While the meringues are baking, make the passionfruit curd. Strain the passionfruit pulp but return a few seeds to it and put it with the remaining ingredients in a heatproof bowl over simmering water. Whisk for 10 minutes or until thickened. Set aside to cool completely, stirring occasionally to prevent a skin from forming.

To serve, top the meringues with a spoon of the lightly whipped cream and a dollop of the passionfruit curd.

NOTE

—

To test to see if the sugar has dissolved in the meringue, rub a small amount of mixture between your fingers; if gritty, keep beating until it feels smooth.

Stuart Scott

SMOKED HAM AND CHEDDAR QUICHETTES WITH GREEN TOMATO PICKLE

Bitesize: Tartlets, Quichettes and Cute Things

The tart green tomato pickle in this recipe brings these gorgeous ham and cheese quichettes alive. We have provided a shortcrust pastry recipe, but you can buy ready-made pastry if you prefer.

MAKES 24
—

250–300 g double-smoked ham, finely diced
200 g cheddar cheese, finely grated
2 large eggs
60 ml pouring cream
fresh thyme leaves to garnish

GREEN TOMATO PICKLE
—

500 g green tomatoes, finely diced
2 small onions, finely diced
3 tablespoons salt
1 teaspoon yellow mustard seeds
¼ teaspoon ground turmeric
1 cinnamon stick
6 cloves
200 ml white vinegar
150 g caster sugar

SHORTCRUST PASTRY
—

300 g plain flour
180 g cold unsalted butter, cubed
pinch of salt
1 egg yolk

For the pastry, place the flour, butter and salt in a food processor and pulse until the mixture resembles breadcrumbs. Add the egg yolk and 2 tablespoons cold water and pulse again until just starting to come together. Knead on a floured work surface to bring together, shape into a disc, wrap in plastic wrap and refrigerate for 1 hour.

Meanwhile, for the pickle, place the tomato and onion in a large bowl, sprinkle with the salt and leave for 3–4 hours. Rinse off the salt and drain well. Place in a saucepan with the remaining ingredients. Bring to the boil over medium heat, reduce the heat and simmer for 30–40 minutes or until thickened. Pour into a sterilised jar and leave to cool. (The green tomato pickle makes 2 cups and will keep refrigerated for 4–6 weeks.)

Preheat the oven to 180°C. Lightly grease twenty-four 6 x 2 cm fluted or plain tartlet tins. Roll out the pastry to 5 mm thick and, using an 8 cm round cutter, cut out 24 circles. Press each circle into a tin, trimming excess pastry. Place on baking trays and refrigerate for 30 minutes.

To blind bake the cases, line them with baking paper and fill with dried beans, rice or baking weights. Bake for 15–20 minutes, remove the beans and paper and bake for a further 10–15 minutes or until golden and cooked through. Remove and set aside to cool in the tins.

Divide the ham and cheese between the cases. Whisk together the eggs and cream in a jug and pour into the cases. Bake for 15–20 minutes or until golden and set. Cool slightly and remove from the tins.

To serve, top each quiche with 1 teaspoon of pickle and garnish with thyme leaves.

WILD MUSHROOM TARTLETS

MAKES 30–35

—

10 g dried porcini mushrooms

2 tablespoons olive oil

1 onion, finely diced

250 g edible wild mushrooms (*or any other type of mushroom*), sliced

2 garlic cloves, crushed

80 ml white wine

2 tablespoons chopped flat-leaf parsley or basil, plus extra flat-leaf parsley for garnish

sea salt and freshly ground black pepper

35 savoury tart shells

Bitesize: Tartlets, Quichettes and Cute Things

If you can't find edible wild mushrooms at your local greengrocer or farmers' market, you can use any type of mushroom you like. Try a combination of button and Swiss brown.

Pour 250 ml boiling water over the porcini mushrooms and leave for 20 minutes. Drain, reserving the porcini and the soaking liquid.

Heat the oil in a saucepan over medium–high heat, add the onion and cook for 3–4 minutes or until softened and translucent. Add the wild mushrooms and cook, stirring often, for 4–5 minutes or until softened. Add the garlic and porcini and cook for 1–2 minutes or until fragrant. Add the wine and cook until reduced by half. Add the reserved porcini soaking liquid and bring to the boil. Reduce the heat and simmer for 10–15 minutes or until all the liquid has evaporated. Add the chopped parsley and season with salt and pepper.

Spoon the hot mushroom mixture into the tartlet shells. Garnish with the parsley leaves.

LITTLE LEMON YOGHURT CAKES

MAKES 12 SMALL CAKES

—

250 g unsalted butter, softened

200 g caster sugar

4 teaspoons grated lemon zest

4 eggs

50 g plain flour

2 teaspoons baking powder

250 g fine semolina

200 g ground almonds

120 ml lemon juice

120 g plain yoghurt

SYRUP

—

250 ml lemon juice

175 g caster sugar

½ tablespoon brandy

Greg and Lucy Malouf, *Malouf: New Middle Eastern Food*

These moist, tangy cakes are delicious on their own with a cup of coffee, or served with a big blob of thick cream and some fresh berries.

Preheat the oven to 180°C. Thoroughly grease two large six-hole muffin tins or twelve 10 cm rectangular mini-loaf tins.

Cream together the butter, sugar and lemon zest until the mixture is pale and smooth. Beat in the eggs, one by one, ensuring each one is completely incorporated before adding the next. Sift the flour and baking powder over the top, add the semolina and ground almonds and gently fold in. Mix in the lemon juice and yoghurt.

Pour the mixture into the prepared tins so they are two-thirds full. Bake for around 20–30 minutes, or until the cakes are firm to the touch and golden brown.

While the cakes are cooking, make the syrup. Combine the lemon juice, sugar and brandy in a small saucepan and bring to the boil. Reduce the heat and simmer for 5 minutes. Remove the cakes from the oven and pierce them all over with a skewer. Pour the syrup over the hot cakes and allow it to soak in. Leave to cool in the tins before turning out. The cakes will keep well in an airtight container for 2–3 days.

VIETNAMESE COFFEE TART WITH FRESH POMEGRANATE

Luke Nguyen, *The Food of Vietnam*

SERVES 6

—

170 g plain flour

¼ teaspoon sea salt

100 g chilled unsalted butter, cut into 1 cm cubes

1½ tablespoons caster sugar

1 teaspoon lemon juice

1 tablespoon cold water

1 pomegranate

VIETNAMESE COFFEE CURD

—

3 eggs

40 g caster sugar

2 teaspoons agar agar

50 ml freshly brewed Vietnamese coffee or strong espresso coffee

3 tablespoons sweetened condensed milk

Sift the flour and salt into a large mixing bowl. Rub in the butter using your fingertips until the mixture has an even sandy texture. Make a well in the centre, then add the sugar, lemon juice and cold water. Lightly mix to form a smooth paste, taking care not to overwork the pastry, so it doesn't shrink during cooking, and adding just a little more cold water if needed to bring it together. Shape the pastry into a round disc, wrap in plastic wrap and refrigerate for 20 minutes.

Divide the pastry into six equal portions. Working quickly, roll each pastry portion out separately to about 3 mm thick. Cut out six 11 cm diameter discs using a round pastry cutter. Ease the pastry discs into six greased 8 cm flan tins, taking care not to stretch the pastry.

Cover the pastry with sheets of foil and weigh the foil down evenly using baking beads or uncooked rice. Rest for 20 minutes in the refrigerator.

Meanwhile, preheat the oven to 190°C.

Bake the tart shells for 20 minutes, then remove the foil and baking beads. Turn the oven down to 170°C and bake for a further 10–15 minutes, or until the pastry is an even golden brown colour. Remove the tart shells from the tins and transfer to a wire rack to cool.

For the Vietnamese coffee curd, beat the eggs in a stainless steel mixing bowl. Add the sugar and beat until the sugar has dissolved. Sprinkle the agar agar into the mixture and whisk again to incorporate. Stir in the coffee and condensed milk. Place the bowl over a saucepan of gently simmering water, ensuring the bottom of the bowl does not touch the water. Continue whisking until the mixture thickens, scraping down the side of the bowl with a spatula occasionally so it doesn't become grainy. Pour into a chilled container to cool, placing some plastic wrap directly on top of the curd to prevent a skin forming.

When the curd is completely cool, pipe it into the cooled tart shells.

Cut the pomegranate in half. Over a bowl, tap the pomegranate with the back of a spoon to release the seeds. Spoon the seeds over the tarts and serve.

NOTE

—

Vietnamese coffee beans are available from gourmet coffee suppliers.

PISTACHIO CHOUX BUNS

April Carter, *Decorated*

These bite-sized choux buns make a cute centrepiece for an afternoon tea or dinner party dessert and aren't as much work as their croquembouche cousin. Once baked, the empty choux buns can be frozen: just pop them in the oven for 5 minutes once they've defrosted to crisp them up. Try these filled with sweetened whipped cream and dipped in chocolate for classic profiteroles or piped into éclair shapes.

MAKES 24

—

70 g plain flour
1 teaspoon caster sugar
¼ teaspoon salt
55 g unsalted butter
2 eggs

PISTACHIO CREAM FILLING

—

70 g pistachio nuts,
    finely ground
2 tablespoons icing sugar
200 ml double cream

GLAZE

—

250 g instant fondant icing
green paste or gel food colouring

TO DECORATE

—

30 g pistachio nuts, roughly
    chopped
edible gold sprinkles

Preheat the oven to 200°C and line two baking trays with baking paper. Sift the flour, sugar and salt into a bowl. Warm the butter with 150 ml water in a large saucepan over a very low heat until the butter has melted. Increase the heat and bring to the boil. Remove from the heat and immediately beat in the flour mixture until there are no lumps. Set aside to cool until just warm.

In a jug, beat the eggs. Gradually add the eggs to the flour mixture, beating constantly until the mixture is smooth, glossy and will drop off a spoon after 3–4 seconds. Transfer the choux mixture to a piping bag fitted with a 1 cm plain nozzle and pipe 24 small buns on to your prepared baking trays at least 2 cm apart. Bake in the oven for 15–25 minutes or until risen, golden brown and crisp. Remove the buns from the oven and make a small hole in the base of each one with a skewer to release the moisture from inside. Return the buns, upside down, to the oven for another 5 minutes then cool on a wire rack.

For the pistachio cream filling, whisk all the ingredients together in a clean bowl until the cream holds its shape.

For the glaze, mix the instant fondant icing with 3–3½ tablespoons warm water and a small amount of food colouring until just runny enough to coat the buns.

Assemble the choux buns just before serving. Fill the piping bag fitted with a 5 mm plain nozzle with the pistachio cream and fill each choux bun. Coat with the fondant and top with some of the roughly chopped pistachio nuts or a single gold sprinkle.

ROSE AND POPPY SEED CAKE

Lucy Cufflin, *Lucy's Bakes*

I lived in France for many years and came across a 'learn English' book, which described an English afternoon tea. It was cake, tea and sandwiches but it was presented in a cottage garden surrounded by climbing roses. I lived in the mountains so the only way to try and recreate this idyll for some neighbours who came for tea was to add the rose to my cake! I have since sourced some wonderful edible rose petals on the internet and scatter my cake with these.

MAKES 1 CAKE

—

4 eggs
caster sugar
self-raising flour
butter and margarine,
    at room temperature
pinch of salt
50 g poppy seeds
1 tablespoon rosewater

ROSE BUTTERCREAM

—

75 g white chocolate
300 g icing sugar, sifted
200 g butter, at room
    temperature
a few drops of pink food
    colouring
3 teaspoons rosewater
edible rose petals to garnish

Preheat the oven to 180°C. Line a 23 cm deep cake tin with baking paper.

Weigh the eggs in their shells and then weigh the same amount of sugar, flour and half the weight in butter and half in margarine.

Beat the butter and margarine together with the sugar in a bowl using a wooden spoon or electric whisk. Beat in 1 egg at a time.

Sift the flour and salt over, then sprinkle in the poppy seeds and rosewater. Gently fold in with a metal spoon.

Turn the cake mix out into the prepared tin and bake for 30 minutes or until risen, browned and springy to the touch, or a skewer inserted in the centre comes out clean.

Turn it out onto a wire rack, remove the paper and leave to cool.

Meanwhile, for the rose buttercream, melt the chocolate in a bowl over a saucepan of boiling water then let it cool for at least 10 minutes. This must not be hot when you make the buttercream. Add the icing sugar, butter, colouring and rosewater and beat until light and fluffy.

Cut the cake in half horizontally and sandwich it back together with a third of the buttercream. Spread the rest over the top and around the side of the cake and scatter with edible rose petals.

Jacqui Melville

DOUBLE CHOCOLATE WHOOPIE PIES

Bitesize: Macarons, Cake Pops and Cute Things

We just had to include something with chocolate, and these double chocolate whoopie pies are the business. Originating from America, whoopie pies consist of two soft and chewy small cake-like cookies sandwiched together with a luscious cream filling.

MAKES 12

—

150 g plain flour
60 g cocoa powder
½ teaspoon bicarbonate of soda
145 g caster sugar
90 g unsalted butter, at room
    temperature
1 teaspoon natural vanilla extract
1 egg
250 ml milk

CHOCOLATE BUTTERCREAM

—

3 egg whites
145 g caster sugar
160 g unsalted butter, cubed
    and at room temperature
125 g dark chocolate (65% *cocoa
    solids*), melted
2 tablespoons cocoa powder

Preheat the oven to 175°C. Grease and flour two baking trays – or three whoopie pie tins. Sift the flour, cocoa and bicarbonate of soda together into a large bowl. Place the sugar and butter in the bowl of a stand mixer and beat on medium speed for 2–3 minutes or until light and creamy. Add the vanilla extract and egg and beat for a further minute. Reduce the speed and add the flour mixture, in three batches, alternating with the milk and beat until combined, scraping down the side of the bowl as required.

Place 1½ tablespoon amounts of batter about 5 cm apart on the trays and bake for 8–10 minutes or until cooked through. Cool for 5 minutes on the trays, then transfer to wire racks to cool completely.

Meanwhile, for the chocolate buttercream, place the egg whites and sugar in the top of a double boiler over medium heat and whisk for 3–4 minutes or until warm and the sugar has dissolved. Remove from the heat. Using electric beaters, beat the mixture on medium–high speed for 6–7 minutes or until glossy and stiff peaks form. Reduce the speed and add the butter, one cube at a time, beating well after each addition. Continue to beat for 2–3 minutes. Combine the melted chocolate and cocoa. Add to the egg white mixture and beat to combine.

Transfer to a piping bag fitted with a 1 cm plain nozzle and pipe 2 tablespoons of filling onto half of the cookies. Sandwich with the remaining cookies.

Marina Oliphant

PUMPKIN DOUGHNUT MUFFINS

Tom Hunt, *The Natural Cook*

These scrummy little muffins are made from a simple variation on a doughnut batter that tastes divine rolled in cinnamon sugar. Baking them in the oven is both much healthier and simpler than deep-frying. The pumpkin gives them an appetising orange colour and keeps them nice and moist.

MAKES 12

—

75 g butter, softened, plus extra for the tin and to brush

180 g spelt flour, plus extra for the tin

75 g rapadura sugar, plus more to coat (*or 75 g raw cane sugar*), plus extra to coat

1 large egg, lightly beaten

1½ teaspoons baking powder

¼ teaspoon bicarbonate of soda

½ teaspoon allspice (*optional*)

3 tablespoons plain live yoghurt

1 teaspoon ground cinnamon

PURÉED PUMPKIN

—

200 g pumpkin

For the puréed pumpkin, peel the pumpkin with a sharp knife or a vegetable peeler. Remove the seeds with a spoon and reserve, then cut the pumpkin roughly into 2–3 cm pieces. Place in a small saucepan and cover with water, bring to the boil, then reduce the heat and simmer for 10–15 minutes until soft.

Strain and reserve the liquid. Put the pumpkin in a blender (make sure it is not more than one-third full) and blend to a purée, adding a little of the cooking liquid to help it become smooth.

Preheat the oven to 180°C. Butter 12 holes of a muffin tin, then sprinkle with flour and turn the tin, tapping, so the holes are well floured.

Beat the butter and sugar for a few minutes until light and fluffy. Add the egg, flour, baking powder, bicarbonate of soda, allspice (if using), yoghurt and pumpkin and stir together until thoroughly mixed.

Fill the muffin holes half full, then bake for 20–25 minutes until springy. Turn out of the tin. Immediately melt a little butter and, as soon as the muffins are cool enough to handle, brush the tops with butter, then roll in a plate of sugar mixed with the cinnamon.

The muffins are best served warm straight from the oven, but will keep for 3 days in an airtight container.

NOTE

—

Rapadura sugar is made from the pure juice extracted from sugar cane. It is available at health food stores and some supermarkets.

Laura Edwards

SUNDAY ROAST

Leisurely weekend lunches are the best kind. And the roast wins points for relative ease and all-round appeal. Accompany it with some buttery, garlicky vegetables and a big bowl of golden potatoes, and you have yourself a relaxed feast.

This chapter includes a selection of roast meat recipes, flavoured and fashioned with spices, sauces, rubs and marinades, together with some easy yet impressive starters and sides.

Try Alain Ducasse's roast chicken cooked with garlic and herbs, and serve it with Justin North's caramelised parsnips, or Daniel Wilson's slow-roasted crushed potatoes (these should become a fast favourite).

For dessert, consider Skye Gyngell's lemon syllabub, or the fruity deliciousness of Jane Kennedy's rhubarb and strawberry crumble.

—

550 g leeks, topped and tailed,
    roughly chopped and rinsed
    thoroughly
400 g medium white floury
    potatoes, scrubbed and
    roughly chopped
250 g onions, roughly chopped
1 garlic clove, crushed
1 litre skim milk
1 litre water
30 ml natural vanilla extract
25 g salt
freshly ground black pepper
    to taste

LEEK, POTATO AND VANILLA SOUP

Gillian, Linsey and Nichola Reith, *Three Sisters Bake*

This soup, made with skim milk, is healthy fare disguised as comfort food. The addition of vanilla brings out the sweetness of the leeks and modernises this old classic.

Put the leeks, potatoes and onion in a large, heavy-based saucepan with the crushed garlic, milk and water. Bring to the boil over high heat, then turn the heat down and simmer for 20 minutes, uncovered. Test the vegetables to ensure they have softened – if the potatoes are still a little hard, simmer for a further 5 minutes. Take the pan off the heat and allow to cool a little before processing the soup with a hand-held blender until smooth. Add the vanilla extract and seasoning and serve.

SERVES 2

—

1 tablespoon sunflower oil
½ large red onion, finely chopped
2 small celery stalks,
    finely chopped
2 tablespoons wholegrain
    mustard
juice of ½ lemon

SALAD

—

250 g asparagus spears, tough
    lower stems removed
½ large tart apple, such as
    granny smith
1 large pear
1 teaspoon sunflower oil
20 g salted butter
½ teaspoon finely chopped
    rosemary
40 g rocket
40 g watercress
50 g mild blue cheese, such
    as gorgonzola
1 large avocado
40 g walnuts, chopped

WARM DOUBLE PEAR SALAD WITH BLUE CHEESE AND WALNUTS

Randi Glenn, *Thrive on Five*

This classic combination of sweet pear, tangy blue cheese and crunchy walnuts has been enhanced with rocket and creamy avocado to make a really luxurious dish. If you like stronger cheese, you could use roquefort or stilton.

To make a dressing, heat the oil in a frying pan and fry the onion and celery for about 7–10 minutes until soft. Add the mustard and lemon juice and set aside.

Meanwhile, for the salad, cook the asparagus in gently simmering water for 2–3 minutes. Drain and pat dry.

Core the apple and pear and cut into 5 mm slices. Heat the 1 teaspoon of oil in a large frying pan, add the slices and cook for 2 minutes, turning carefully halfway through.

Preheat the grill to a medium setting. In a separate ovenproof frying pan, heat the butter until golden. Add the rosemary and asparagus. Sauté for a couple of minutes before adding half the rocket and half the watercress. Mix briefly and crumble the cheese over the top. Place under the grill for about 3 minutes, until the cheese has melted and the asparagus is glazed.

Now arrange the salad by placing the remaining rocket and watercress in a bowl. Slice the avocado and place on top, then add the lukewarm apple and pear slices. Top with the warm asparagus and cheese mixture, spoon over the dressing and finish with the chopped walnuts. Serve warm.

Dan Jones

ROAST DUCK WITH POMEGRANATE GLAZE

Adrian Richardson, *Meat*

Most people know that sour, tangy fruits, such as orange and cherries, go brilliantly with duck's rich, dark meat. I also like to use pomegranate, a slightly more unusual fruit, which has a distinctive sweet–sour tang and complements duck perfectly. Don't worry about trying to get hold of fresh pomegranates. Pomegranate syrup (also called molasses) is available throughout the year from specialist food stores and Middle Eastern grocers. It's dark and sticky and is easy to make into a glaze. Because it caramelises quickly, don't start basting the ducks until about three-quarters of the way through the cooking time. Substitute ripe nectarines for the pears when they are in season. The pickled onion is a quick and easy sort of pickle, which is more about softening the harshness of the raw onions than preserving them for any length of time.

SERVES 4

—

2 x 1.8 kg ducks
salt
freshly ground black pepper
1 onion, quartered
1 orange, quartered
4 garlic cloves, sliced
1 bunch thyme
5 tablespoons pomegranate
  molasses
80 ml olive oil
2 bunches watercress, leaves
  picked
4 ripe pears, sliced
pomegranate seeds (*optional*)

QUICK PICKLED ONION

—

30 ml red wine vinegar
½ teaspoon salt
1½ red onions, thinly sliced
1½ tablespoons extra-virgin
  olive oil
½ cup parsley leaves
¼ cup coriander leaves
1 tablespoon ground sumac
¼ teaspoon freshly ground
  black pepper

For the quick pickled onion, combine the vinegar and salt in a large mixing bowl and stir until dissolved. Add the onions and stir so that they are covered with the pickling mixture. Cover with plastic wrap and leave to soak for 2 hours. In another small bowl, mix the olive oil with the fresh herbs, sumac and pepper. Remove the onions from the pickling mixture and stir into the oil. Serve straight away or refrigerate for up to 1 week.

Preheat the oven to 200°C. Remove the ducks' necks (if still attached) and trim away any loose fat. Cut off the first wing joints and remove any giblets from inside the birds. Season each cavity generously with salt and pepper. Divide the onion, orange, garlic and thyme evenly between the birds, tucking them snugly inside the cavities. Drizzle 1 tablespoon of pomegranate molasses into each bird then use a long piece of butcher's string to tie the back legs to the parson's nose. This will seal the cavity and flavour the bird from the inside.

Place the ducks on a rack inside a large roasting tin and rub them all over with olive oil. Season generously and roast in the centre of the oven for 1–1½ hours, depending on your oven.

Every 15 minutes or so during roasting, remove the ducks from the oven (not forgetting to close the oven door, to maintain the cooking temperature) and tip the roasting tin on an angle, so that the fat pools in the corner. Baste the ducks all over, being a little careful, as the hot fat may sizzle and spit.

Three-quarters of the way through the cooking time, carefully tip off about ¼ cup of the hot duck fat and mix it with the remaining 3 tablespoons of pomegranate molasses to make a glaze. Stir well and brush onto the ducks. Repeat several times until the ducks are cooked a rich dark brown, reserving a little of the glaze for serving.

Transfer the cooked ducks to a hot plate and leave them to rest for 10 minutes in a warm spot. To serve, use kitchen scissors or a cleaver to cut the birds into portions on the bone.

Pile the duck pieces onto a large serving platter and top with the watercress, pears and pickled onion. Drizzle with a little of the reserved pomegranate glaze and scatter over a few pomegranate seeds (if using).

Dean Cambray

SLOW-ROASTED CRUSHED POTATOES AND GARLIC

Daniel Wilson, *Huxtabook*

This is my version of roast potatoes — another dish that is popular at our house. The secret is good-quality potatoes and olive oil. The trick to these potatoes is that when you break them up with your hands, make sure you have bits of all different sizes, so that when they're cooked some are crispy and some are soft. They're excellent for soaking up sauces.

SERVES 4

—

1 kg small roasting potatoes, such as nicola or king edward, washed well
20 garlic cloves, peeled and brown end bits removed
sea salt
freshly ground black pepper
200 ml extra-virgin olive oil

Preheat the oven to 175°C.

Place the potatoes in a large saucepan of salted cold water. Bring to a boil, then reduce the heat and simmer for 30 minutes, or until soft. Drain in a colander and leave to cool.

Crush the potatoes with your hands into a large bowl, leaving some chunks the size of a walnut, and others smaller than that.

Add the garlic cloves and olive oil and toss together. Season with sea salt and freshly ground black pepper and toss again.

Place the potatoes and garlic cloves in a roasting tin, spreading them evenly in one layer. Roast for 40–50 minutes, or until golden and crisp, turning every 15 minutes.

Serve hot in a large bowl.

Chris Middleton

BALINESE SLOW-ROASTED PORK

Leanne Kitchen and Antony Suvalko, *East*

This is a very famous dish from Indonesia, which goes by the name *babi guling*, meaning 'roast pork'. Usually a pig around 12 months old is traditionally cooked over hot coals for 3–4 hours. If you get the chance to visit Bali, get along to a babi guling restaurant – it's an unforgettable local dining experience. This recipe calls for kencur, which is a ginger-like tuber with a very strong, medicinal flavour. It's easiest to buy it ground from Asian supermarkets. Serve this with plain boiled rice and a nice cold beer! Because you need to refrigerate the pork for at least 8 hours, you will need to start this the day before you plan to serve it.

SERVES 8
—

1.5 kg piece boneless pork belly
1½ tablespoons salt
1 teaspoon ground turmeric
1 tablespoon vegetable oil
kecap manis to serve
peanut crackers (*optional*)
    to serve
lime wedges to serve

TOMATO SAMBAL
—

2 teaspoons belacan
    (*Malaysian shrimp paste*)
1 onion, finely chopped
8 garlic cloves, finely chopped
12 large red chillies, seeded
    and sliced
2 tablespoons vegetable oil
600 g very ripe tomatoes,
    finely chopped
1 tablespoon sugar

For the tomato sambal, wrap the belacan in foil. Heat a small, heavy-based frying pan over medium heat, add the wrapped belacan then dry-fry for 2 minutes on each side, or until fragrant. Cool and unwrap.

In a saucepan over medium heat, cook the onion, garlic and chilli in the oil, stirring, for 4–5 minutes or until the onion has softened. Add the belacan, tomatoes and sugar and bring to a simmer. Cook, stirring often, for 30 minutes or until reduced and thickened.

Transfer to a food processor and process until a coarse paste forms. Season to taste with salt and freshly ground black pepper. Cool to room temperature. (The sambal will keep, stored in an airtight container in the refrigerator, for up to 1 week.)

For the spice paste, wrap the trasi in foil. Heat a small, heavy-based frying pan over medium heat, add the wrapped trasi then dry-fry for 2 minutes on each side, or until fragrant. Cool and unwrap. Combine with the remaining paste ingredients in a food processor and process until a fairly smooth paste forms. Alternatively, use a mortar and pestle.

Using a sharp knife, score the underside of the pork belly all over in a criss-cross pattern, cutting about 1 cm into the meat.

Rub the paste all over the scored pork flesh then place in a non-reactive dish, skin side up.

Combine the salt, ground turmeric and oil. Using your fingers, rub this all over the skin of the pork. Refrigerate the meat for 8 hours or overnight for the flavours to develop and the skin to dry out.

SPICE PASTE

—

1½ teaspoons trasi
 (*Indonesian shrimp paste*)

3 lemongrass stems, white part
 only, chopped

5 kaffir lime leaves, central vein
 removed, finely chopped

3 candlenuts, coarsely chopped
 (*see notes*)

5 brown shallots, coarsely
 chopped

4 garlic cloves, chopped

6 red bird's eye chillies

1 tablespoon chopped fresh
 turmeric or 1 teaspoon
 ground turmeric

3 cm piece fresh ginger,
 chopped

3 teaspoons ground coriander

3 teaspoons ground kencur

1½ tablespoons vegetable oil

Remove the pork from the refrigerator and bring to room temperature. Preheat the oven to 180°C.

Roast the belly, skin side up, for 25 minutes. Remove the pork from the oven and prick the skin all over with a thin metal skewer, then roast for another 25 minutes.

Heat the oven grill to high and put the pork, skin side up, on an oven tray lined with foil. Cook under the grill, about 8–10 cm from the heat, for 10–12 minutes or until the skin is evenly crackled – you may need to rotate the pork to get an even crackling. If you don't have a grill, you can cook the crackling in a 230°C oven for 15–20 minutes or until crisp.

Stand the pork at room temperature for 10–15 minutes to rest the meat, then slice into 1 cm thick pieces. Serve immediately with some kecap manis and tomato sambal for dipping, peanut crackers (if using) and lime wedges for squeezing over.

NOTES

—

candlenuts are hard nuts from a flowering tree, which have a high oil content. They are used, ground, to thicken (mainly) Malaysian and Indonesian curries. They are toxic raw, so should always be cooked.

peanut crackers These are Javanese-style crackers, known as *rempeyek* or *peyek*, can be found in Asian grocery stores or online.

shrimp paste is a common ingredient in Southeast Asian cuisine, and comes in many guises, all of them reasonably pungent. Shrimp paste lends a distinctive background flavour to spice pastes and sauces and will last a long time if you keep it refrigerated. As it's quite strong, it is used in small quantities. Belacan is the Malaysian version and is sold in a solid block. Trasi is the name for Indonesian shrimp paste, also sold in a block. Both these types are raw and require toasting in foil before using.

SLOW-ROASTED LAMB SHOULDER WITH HARISSA

Brent Owens, *Dig In!*

This is my take on the Aussie classic, roast lamb. I've added interest by slow-cooking and then shredding the meat, and serving it with a spicy harissa. There is also a cooling mint and yoghurt dip for freshness. Serve with flatbreads.

SERVES 4–6

—

2 kg lamb shoulder, bone in
lemon wedges to serve
mint leaves to serve

HARISSA

—

10 long red chillies,
    roughly chopped
3 garlic cloves, peeled
1 teaspoon ground cumin
½ teaspoon ground caraway
1 teaspoon ground coriander
½ teaspoon salt
2 tablespoons olive oil

MINT AND YOGHURT DIP

—

juice of ½ lemon
handful of chopped mint
250 g Greek-style yoghurt

Preheat the oven to 180°C.

For the harissa, put the chillies, garlic, spices, salt and olive oil in a blender or food processor and blitz to form a fine paste, adding a little water to help it mix, if required. Spread the harissa over the lamb and set aside to marinate for at least 1 hour.

Put 750 ml water in a large roasting tin. Put in a roasting rack and place the lamb on top. Cover the lamb with foil and roast in the oven for 2 hours. After 2 hours, remove the foil and roast for a further 2 hours, or until the lamb can be pulled apart with two forks but still holds its shape.

For the mint and yoghurt dip, combine all the ingredients in a small bowl.

Serve the lamb with the dip, lemon wedges and mint leaves.

ROAST BEEF AND YORKSHIRE PUDDINGS

Rachael Lane, *Great Pub Food*

SERVES 4

—

3 potatoes, quartered

1 kg whole scotch fillet

oil

2 tablespoons wholegrain
    mustard

1 tablespoon chopped thyme

1 tablespoon chopped rosemary

sea salt

freshly ground black pepper

¼ pumpkin, cut into
    5 cm chunks

4 small brown onions

YORKSHIRE PUDDINGS

—

120 g plain flour

½ teaspoon sea salt

250 ml full-cream milk

1 large egg

3 tablespoons lard, vegetable oil
    or melted butter

GRAVY

—

2 tablespoons plain flour

125 ml red wine

250 ml beef stock

Preheat the oven to 220°C. Place a wire rack in a large roasting tin.

Put the potatoes in a saucepan, cover with cold water and bring to the boil. Cook for 5 minutes. Drain.

Cover the beef with oil, mustard, the herbs and salt and pepper, and place on the rack. Put the potatoes, pumpkin and onions around the beef and drizzle with oil. Cook for 15 minutes.

For the Yorkshire pudding batter, sift the flour and salt together in a bowl and make a well in the centre. Lightly beat the milk and egg together and pour this mixture into the well. Whisk to a smooth batter and set aside.

Reduce the oven temperature to 180°C. Cook the beef for 25 minutes, for medium, or until cooked to your liking. Transfer the beef and vegetables onto a tray, cover with foil and keep warm. Set the roasting tin aside for gravy.

Increase the oven temperature to 240°C.

Divide the lard, vegetable or butter oil among four holes of a ¾ cup capacity muffin tin and heat in the oven for 5 minutes or until almost smoking. Carefully remove the tray from the oven. Quickly pour the Yorkshire pudding batter into the prepared muffin holes. Cook for 15 minutes, or until puffed and golden brown.

For the gravy, place the roasting tin over medium heat, add the flour to the meat fat and juices and cook, stirring constantly, for 30 seconds, or until it begins to colour. Pour in the wine and stock and simmer, stirring occasionally and scraping any cooked particles from the base of the tin with a wooden spoon, until the gravy thickens. Add any juices from the rested meat. Strain through a fine-mesh sieve into a gravy boat or heatproof jug, which has been preheated with boiling water.

Carve the beef into thick slices and serve with the roast vegetables, Yorkshire puddings and gravy.

—
1 small celeriac
900 ml whole cow's or goat
   or almond milk
25 g butter *(optional)*

PURÉED CELERIAC WITH BUTTER

Tom Hunt, *The Natural Cook*

Celeriac purée is ultimately decadent, rich and smooth. It goes incredibly well with roast meat, especially lamb.

Prepare the celeriac and cut the white flesh roughly into 2–3 cm cubes. Put it into a small saucepan with the milk and bring to the boil, then reduce the heat to a low simmer for 30 minutes. Check every now and then that the milk is not scorching on the base of the pan.

Test the celeriac by piercing it with a knife to see if it is soft. Allow to cool a little, then ladle into a blender with enough of the milk to make a thick purée (do not fill the blender more than about one-third full – work in batches if necessary). Make sure the lid is secured as the liquid is hot. Blend until very smooth. Return to the pan, add the butter (if using) and season.

This dish will keep well in an airtight container in the refrigerator for 4 days. To serve, reheat gently until piping hot but not boiling.

SERVES 4
—
4 parsnips
vegetable oil
40 g butter

CARAMELISED PARSNIPS

Justin North, *French Lessons*

Peel the parsnips and trim the base end and tip. Slice each parsnip lengthways around its central core into four curved wedges. Cut each wedge in half and slice away any remaining core, which is tough and fibrous.

Heat the oil in a frying pan over medium heat. Add the parsnip batons and sauté for a few minutes until they start to colour. Season well with salt and freshly ground black pepper, add the butter and cook it to a light brown foam. Continue to sauté the parsnips, basting frequently, until they are caramelised to a deep golden brown, about 8–10 minutes.

—

1 small bunch of parsley,
    washed, dried and
    chopped (*stalks reserved*)
1 small bunch of chervil,
    washed, dried and chopped
    (*stalks reserved*)
1 very small bunch of tarragon,
    washed, dried and chopped
    (*stalks reserved*)
2 pink garlic bulbs
pinch of mignonette pepper
100 g strained fromage blanc
    or quark (*see recipe below if
    you'd like to make your own*)
1 good-quality free-range
    chicken
4 thyme sprigs
4 rosemary sprigs
2 tablespoons olive oil

HERBY ROAST CHICKEN

Alain Ducasse, *Nature*

Always choose a good-quality free-range chicken so you can be sure that it has seen the sun and ended its life in semi-freedom. All others, even 'farm fresh' chickens, spend their entire lives in rearing sheds. A herb salad goes particularly well with this chicken and gives you loads of vitamins and minerals as well. Get your butcher to spatchcock the chicken for you (severing the ends of the feet and wings, splitting the back lengthways and flattening it out). Ask him also to crush the neck.

Preheat the oven to 200 °C. Put the parsley, chervil and tarragon leaves in a bowl.

Cut the tops off the two bulbs of pink garlic, then take two garlic cloves from them, chop these and add them to the bowl along with the mignonette pepper and strained fromage blanc. Add salt to taste and mix well. Push this herb preparation under the skin of the chicken through the opening in the neck. Push with your fingers until the flesh of the breast and legs is well covered. Then salt inside the bird.

In a roasting tin, spread out the thyme sprigs, rosemary sprigs and the reserved herb stalks. Lay the chicken on this aromatic bed and distribute around it the giblets and garlic bulbs, with the cut sides down. Brush with the olive oil and roast in the oven for 20 minutes. Then lower the heat to 180°C and take out the garlic bulbs. Cook for a further 20–30 minutes (depending on the size of your chicken), basting fairly regularly. When the chicken is cooked, transfer it to a dish, cover with aluminium foil and allow to rest for 10 minutes.

In the meantime, pour half a glass of water into the roasting tin and scrape up all the juices. Cut up the chicken and arrange the pieces on a serving dish. Drizzle the cooking juices over the chicken or serve separately.

—

100 g cottage cheese
125 g plain yoghurt
3 teaspoons lemon juice

FROMAGE BLANC

Margaret Fulton, *The Encyclopedia of Food and Cookery*

In France, fromage blanc is made from skimmed milk soured with a culture, but you can make an excellent substitute at home by blending together cottage cheese, plain yoghurt and lemon juice.

Place all the ingredients in a food processor or blender, and process thoroughly until the mixture is smooth, shiny and as thick as whipped cream. Cover and store in the refrigerator for 12 hours before using. You may also use a food mill, beating the mixture thoroughly after pushing it through the mill.

Françoise Nicol

SERVES 8

—

200 g caster sugar
200 ml dry sherry
finely grated zest and juice
    of 1 lemon
600 ml double cream
1–2 teaspoons finely chopped
    preserved stem ginger
    in syrup (optional)

LEMON SYLLABUB

Skye Gyngell, *A Year in My Kitchen*

Wonderfully simple in its execution, this delightful dessert requires no technical skill, just willing tastebuds to adjust the flavours if necessary. A little diced stem ginger is a lovely addition if you happen to have any to hand.

Combine the sugar, sherry, lemon zest and juice in a bowl and stir well.

In another bowl, very lightly whip the cream – just enough to thicken it slightly. Gently fold the sherry mixture into the cream until just combined (the addition of lemon and sherry will continue to thicken the cream). At this point, fold in the chopped ginger together with a little of the syrup from the jar (if using).

Spoon the syllabub into small glasses and refrigerate for an hour or so to chill before serving.

SERVES 4

—

4 rhubarb stalks, trimmed
    and cut into small pieces
1½ tablespoons coconut sugar
juice of 1 orange
170 g strawberries, hulled
100 g ground almonds
1 tablespoon flaked coconut
10 g butter
Greek-style yoghurt to serve
    (optional)

RHUBARB AND STRAWBERRY CRUMBLE

Jane Kennedy, *OMG! I Can Eat That?*

Preheat the oven to 180°C. Place the rhubarb, 2 teaspoons of the coconut sugar and the orange juice in a small saucepan and bring to a gentle boil. Simmer for about 10 minutes, or until the rhubarb is soft. You may need to add a little water to make sure the rhubarb stays moist.

Add the strawberries and simmer for a further 5 minutes. Remove from the heat and pour the mixture into four individual ramekins.

Combine the ground almonds, coconut flakes, butter and the remaining coconut sugar and mix with your fingers to create the 'crumble'. Sprinkle a little mixture over each ramekin.

Bake for 20–25 minutes, or until bubbling and browned on top. Serve with a little dollop of Greek-style yoghurt if you like!

Mark Roper

UPSIDE DOWN SALTED CARAMEL CHEESECAKE WITH MACADAMIA PRALINE

Lyndey Milan, *Lyndey Milan's Taste of Australia*

The perennially popular cheesecake is given a modern update with no biscuit base, but rather a moreish praline made with macadamia nuts. I cooked the dish overlooking the beach on a wild and woolly afternoon.

SERVES 4
—

125 ml pouring cream
185 g cream cheese, softened
1 teaspoon vanilla bean paste

SALTED CARAMEL SAUCE
—

60 g butter
110 g muscovado or
    dark brown sugar
125 ml pouring cream
1 teaspoon sea salt flakes
1 teaspoon vanilla bean paste

MACADAMIA PRETZEL PRALINE
—

40 g butter
2 tablespoons maple syrup
55 g icing sugar
70 g macadamia nuts, toasted
    and roughly chopped
½ cup roughly crushed pretzels

For the salted caramel sauce, melt the butter in a medium saucepan, add the sugar and cook for 5 minutes or until the sugar dissolves and starts to turn golden, stirring from time to time. Add the cream and salt and bring to the boil. Boil gently for 10 minutes, whisking occasionally, until thickened. Remove from the heat and pour into a small bowl; add the vanilla and set aside to cool.

For the macadamia pretzel praline, place a medium saucepan over low heat, add the butter and melt, stirring from time to time to distribute the milk solids, and continue to cook until it foams and turns nut brown. Stir in the maple syrup and icing sugar, bring to the boil and cook for 2 minutes. Add the macadamia nuts and crushed pretzels and stir quickly until coated. Spoon onto a baking tray lined with baking paper and set aside to cool. When cool, break into small chunks.

Using an electric mixer, beat the cream until soft peaks form. In a larger bowl, using the same beaters, whip the cream cheese, vanilla and 1 tablespoon of the cooled salted caramel sauce until fluffy. Gently fold through the cream.

Spoon into serving glasses, top with a spoonful of salted caramel sauce and scatter over a few chunks of macadamia pretzel praline. Serve immediately.

This dessert can be made ahead and refrigerated (without the praline) but, for best results, remove it from the refrigerator at least 1 hour before serving sprinkled with the praline.

NOTES
—

muscovado sugar is a type of brown sugar, which may be unrefined or partially unrefined. It is available from health food stores and some supermarkets.

IMPROMPTU DINNER PARTY

The spontaneous dinner with friends might be rare these days, but it doesn't have to be. Next time you have unexpected visitors, make like it's no sweat for them to stay for a meal and look to these recipes as inspiration. You needn't have done any prep or a special shop — maybe give or take a dash to your local.

Anna and Fanny Bergenström's parmesan breadsticks use puff pastry (yes, from the freezer), and are lovely with an aperitif. Or our cover star, bruschetta with broad beans and pecorino, works as a simple starter.

Antonio Carluccio's zabaglione with bitter chocolate sauce comes together quickly, and then really only needs time in the refrigerator to chill — perhaps while guests enjoy Lyndey Milan's seared wagyu with mushroom ragu and zucchini salad, or Anjum Anand's 25-minute cardamom lamb.

EASY PARMESAN BREADSTICKS

frozen puff pastry sheets
lightly beaten egg
grated parmesan

Anna and Fanny Bergenström, *Under the Walnut Tree*

These cheesy breadsticks are prepared using ready-made sheets of puff pastry, and are great with all kinds of creamy soups or with a pre-dinner drink. You can vary the quantities to suit.

If using frozen puff pastry, let it thaw at room temperature for 15–20 minutes. Meanwhile, preheat the oven to 200°C.

Use a rolling pin to roll out the puff pastry just a little (use a bit of flour if needed). Transfer to a baking tray lined with non-stick baking paper. Brush the pastry with lightly beaten egg and sprinkle with grated parmesan. Using a blunt knife or dough scraper, carefully cut the pastry into 2 x 10 cm strips and separate them. Bake for 12–15 minutes, or until golden.

BRUSCHETTA WITH BROAD BEANS AND PECORINO

SERVES 6
—
200 g fresh or frozen baby
     broad beans
½ red chilli, sliced
1 small brown onion,
     roughly chopped
100 g pancetta, cut into
     thin short strips
60 ml olive oil

½ loaf sourdough bread
1 garlic clove, halved
extra-virgin olive oil for drizzling
shaved pecorino to serve

Luca Lorusso and Vivienne Polak, *Sharing Puglia*

Whether served for breakfast, as a snack or light meal, this bruschetta is easy to prepare and rich in flavour and texture. Crunchy, toasted bread and soft, new broad beans are accompanied by shavings of sharp pecorino, an anointing of extra-virgin olive oil and finished off with salty pancetta. If using frozen broad beans, defrost them first. Slip the skins off the beans and place them in a bowl.

Blanch the broad beans for 5 minutes in boiling salted water and drain.

In a frying pan over medium heat, sauté the chilli, onion and pancetta in 2 tablespoons of the olive oil for 5 minutes.

Meanwhile, heat a chargrill pan over high heat or a barbecue to high, and brush it lightly with the remaining olive oil.

Slice the bread into six thick slices and place it on the preheated chargrill pan or barbecue. Leave the bread undisturbed for a few minutes, until it is golden and there are griddle marks on it. Turn and cook the other sides. Once the bread is toasted, rub the garlic vigorously over both sides of the bruschetta. Place one slice of bruschetta on each plate, and top with some of the blanched broad beans and sautéed pancetta mixture. Season to taste and drizzle a little extra-virgin olive oil over each piece. Top with the shaved pecorino and serve.

Alicia Taylor

Alan Benson

SERVES 4

—

4 firm peaches (*or rockmelon*),
  preferably in peak season
300 ml extra-virgin olive oil
4 small or 2 large buffalo
  mozzarella balls, torn into
  bite-sized pieces
16 thin slices prosciutto
wild rocket to garnish
crusty bread to serve

GRILLED PEACH, WARM MOZZARELLA AND PROSCIUTTO

Stefano de Pieri and Jim McDougall, *Nuovo Mondo*

This dish is about as easy to prepare as it gets, but relies completely on the quality of the ingredients. If the ingredients you source are the best available, the dish will sing.

Preheat a chargrill pan until it is smoking hot. Stand a peach up on a chopping board with the stem end facing up and slice off the cheeks. (There will be a bit of wastage but you can dice the remaining flesh and sprinkle it over the salad, or just eat it on the spot.) Repeat for each peach. Rub a little olive oil onto the cut surface of each peach cheek and grill for about 20 seconds on each side, or until there are lovely grill marks on the peach.

Heat the olive oil in a small saucepan over low heat for about 5 minutes. Add the mozzarella and continue to heat for a further 2 minutes. Remove from the heat and let it sit so the mozzarella warms through.

Arrange the grilled peach on serving plates. Remove the mozzarella from the oil and arrange a few pieces on each plate. Place the prosciutto on top – the prosciutto lets you give height to the dish when plating, so be creative. Garnish with rocket and spoon some of the warm oil over the salad. This dish is best eaten with some good crusty bread.

SERVES 4

—

1 teaspoon coriander seeds
½ teaspoon cumin seeds
2 tablespoons coconut or
  vegetable oil
10 curry leaves
1 onion, sliced
2.5 cm piece fresh ginger, grated
4 green chillies, slit lengthways
½ teaspoon ground turmeric
500 ml coconut milk
sea salt
25 g caster sugar
1 teaspoon chilli flakes
500 g king scallops
1 tablespoon vegetable oil

SCALLOPS WITH COCONUT AND GINGER

Reza Mahammad, *Reza's Indian Spice*

An easy dish which takes just minutes. The sauce here is very south Indian in inspiration, based on a moilee. You could use it with prawns as well, to delicious effect.

Place the coriander and cumin seeds in a dry frying pan and toast until golden and wonderfully fragrant. Remove to a mortar and crush them with a pestle. Set aside.

Heat the coconut oil in a large frying pan, add the curry leaves, onion, ginger and chillies. Cook and stir until the onion is soft, then add the turmeric, followed by the coconut milk, sea salt and sugar. Bring to a simmer and cook for 3–5 minutes, until the sauce turns glossy and thickens enough to coat the back of the spoon. Keep warm.

Mix together the ground, toasted coriander and cumin seeds and the chilli flakes and coat the scallops to give an even crust. Heat the vegetable oil in a large frying pan until hot, then add the scallops. Sear for about 1 minute on each side until golden, sprinkle salt on each and remove from the pan. Serve with the warm sauce. These would be lovely served on top of a mound of spinach.

—

4 x 180 g wagyu steaks
1 tablespoon extra-virgin olive oil

MUSHROOM RAGU

—

30 g butter
100 g saffron milk cap (*pine*)
  mushrooms or Swiss brown
  or portobello mushrooms,
  cleaned
4 thyme sprigs
80 ml chicken stock

ZUCCHINI SALAD

—

2 zucchini
grated zest and juice of 1 lemon
60 ml extra-virgin olive oil
1 garlic clove, finely chopped
1 large red chilli, seeded and
  finely chopped
¼ cup mint leaves, torn

SEARED WAGYU WITH MUSHROOM RAGU AND ZUCCHINI SALAD

Lyndey Milan, *Lyndey Milan's Taste of Australia*

This looks impressive, but it takes just 10 minutes to prepare and 15 minutes to cook.

For the mushroom ragu, melt the butter in a medium frying pan over medium heat until it starts to foam. Add the saffron milk cap mushrooms (torn in half if large and wiped clean with a cloth) and cook for a minute or so. Add the thyme sprigs, chicken stock and season to taste with salt and freshly ground black pepper. Cook for 7–8 minutes, stirring occasionally, until the mushrooms are soft and the stock has evaporated.

For the zucchini salad, using a vegetable peeler or sharp knife, shave the zucchini into thin strips. Combine the lemon zest and juice, oil, garlic and chilli in a bowl and whisk. Season to taste with salt and freshly ground black pepper.

To cook the wagyu, heat a frying pan over medium heat. Season the steaks with salt and pepper. Add the oil to the frying pan and, after 30 seconds, add the steaks. Cook for 1–2 minutes on each side or until cooked as desired. Remove and rest in a warm place for 5 minutes.

To serve, pour the dressing over the zucchini and toss gently to combine then top with the torn mint leaves. Serve with the wagyu and mushroom ragu.

SERVES 4

—

1 large cucumber, peeled
  and cut into chunks
2 tablespoons dill,
  finely chopped
3 tablespoons double cream
2 large beefsteak tomatoes,
  skinned and chopped
10 basil leaves, plus extra
  to garnish
1 white onion, peeled and
  roughly chopped

RAW CUCUMBER AND TOMATO SOUP

Antonio Carluccio, *Simple Cooking*

For this soup, the ingredients are raw, and the mixture of the two soups and two colours is spectacular to look at. It is a delightfully refreshing dish for a hot summer's day! For extra colour and texture, try adding a tablespoon of very finely chopped mixed tomato and cucumber to each serving.

Purée the cucumber with the dill in a blender or food processor. Add the cream and season to taste with a little salt and freshly ground black pepper. Chill in the refrigerator Process the skinned tomatoes with the basil and onion. Season to taste and chill in the refrigerator. To serve, first put the cucumber soup in a deep soup plate, then carefully add the tomato soup in the centre and garnish with a few basil leaves.

Alastair Hendy

SERVES 6

—

2 fresh tuna steaks
    (about 200 g each)
80 g sesame seeds
80 g black sesame seeds
sea salt and freshly ground
    black pepper
2 tablespoons olive oil
lime wedges to serve

WASABI MAYONNAISE

1 tablespoon light mayonnaise
1 tablespoon Greek-style
    yoghurt
wasabi paste to taste

SESAME TUNA SQUARES

Jane Kennedy, *OMG! I Can Eat That?*

A combination of sesame seeds gives these nibbles a great crunch and the wasabi mayo gives the tuna a zingy bite.

Cut the tuna into approximately 3 cm squares. Sprinkle both the sesame seeds on a large plate. Season the tuna squares with sea salt and pepper. Roll the squares in the sesame mix.

Heat the olive oil in a large non-stick frying pan over medium heat. Using tongs, gently place the tuna squares in the pan. Cook on one side for 1½ minutes, then turn and cook for another minute. Do the same on all sides. Place on paper towel.

To make the wasabi mayonnaise, combine all the ingredients in a small bowl.

Sprinkle the tuna squares with sea salt and pepper. Serve with lime wedges and the wasabi mayonnaise.

SERVES 4–6

—

1.5 kg chicken thighs or breasts,
    skin on, cut into plum-sized
    morsels
plain flour for coating
salt and pepper
120 ml olive oil
1 onion, finely chopped
50 ml dry white wine

SAUCE

—

2 whole eggs, beaten together
    with 2 extra egg yolks
juice of 1 lemon
1 garlic clove, peeled and puréed
1 tablespoon parsley, finely
    chopped

CHICKEN WITH LEMON AND EGG SAUCE

Antonio Carluccio, *Simple Cooking*

You can use young spring lamb instead of the chicken, but just cook it for a bit longer – about another 20 minutes.

Dust all the pieces of chicken with flour seasoned with salt and pepper, shaking off the surplus.

Heat the olive oil in a frying pan until it nearly sizzles, add the onion and fry gently until soft, about 10 minutes. Add the chicken and, stirring occasionally, cook for 20 minutes until browned on all sides. Pour in the wine and cook gently for another 20 minutes. When the chicken is cooked, remove the pan from the heat.

Meanwhile, mix together the eggs, lemon juice, garlic, plenty of freshly ground pepper and the parsley, seasoning to taste with salt. Pour this mixture on to the chicken while still hot. Stir to coat all the pieces of chicken: the sauce should just thicken without becoming scrambled egg (rather similar to a spaghetti carbonara).

Mark Roper

—

600 g regular or baby eggplants
salt
1 garlic clove, finely chopped
80–100 ml olive oil, plus extra
    if necessary
100–200 g crumbled feta,
    depending on the size of
    the eggplants
chopped parsley leaves to serve
    (optional)

EGGPLANT BAKED WITH FETA

Rebecca Seal, *The Islands of Greece*

This is a deceptively simple dish. The combination of roasted eggplant, garlic and feta, with a little olive oil, is perfect. You can easily increase the quantities to make this a main, rather than a starter.

Preheat the oven to 200°C.

Cut the eggplants in half, then run a knife along the middle of the flesh lengthways, but not all the way through to the skin. Do the same, making a shorter cut, parallel to the central cut, on both sides. Lay the eggplants in a baking dish, cut side up, and sprinkle with a pinch of salt. Press the garlic into the cuts and drizzle generously with the oil (use a little extra if they look dry). Finally, top each with some of the feta.

Bake in the oven for 15–25 minutes, depending on size. They are cooked when the eggplants are beginning to collapse and the feta is just browning. Serve scattered with a little parsley.

SERVES 4

—

10 g unsalted butter
2 teaspoons extra-virgin olive oil
20 raw king prawns, peeled and
    deveined
1 red chilli, finely diced
    (seeded if you prefer less heat)
1 lime plus the grated zest and
    juice of ½ lime
1 tablespoon roughly chopped
    coriander leaves

FIERY PRAWNS

Gillian, Linsey and Nichola Reith, *Three Sisters Bake*

As well as being an essential part of the seafood platter, these prawns make a really good, quick pasta dish. Toss some pasta in olive oil, mix through some chopped cherry tomatoes and top with the prawns.

Heat the butter and oil in a shallow frying pan over high heat until the butter is foaming. Fry the king prawns in the pan for 2 minutes, stirring them occasionally. After 2 minutes, add the chilli, lime zest and juice and cook for a further 2 minutes. Immediately remove them from the pan, toss through the coriander and serve.

Steven Joyce

Lisa Linder

SERVES 3
—

1½ tablespoons plain yoghurt

1 smallish tomato, quartered

10 g fresh ginger, coarsely chopped (*peeled weight*)

2 large garlic cloves

1 rounded teaspoon ground coriander

1 teaspoon ground cardamom, or to taste

1 teaspoon ground cumin

60 ml vegetable oil

1 onion, finely chopped

1–2 green chillies, pierced with the tip of a knife

200 ml lamb or chicken stock, or water

350 g lamb rump, trimmed and cut into 2.5 cm chunks

EASY 25-MINUTE CARDAMOM LAMB

Anjum Anand, *Anjum's Quick and Easy Indian*

A lovely, light lamb curry inspired by Sindhi cardamom chicken curries. The flavours are delicate but quite wonderful and it cooks in less than 30 minutes. For quickest results, cook the curry in an open, wide pan so that there is more surface area for the ingredients to cook.

Blend together the yoghurt, tomato, ginger, garlic and ground spices until smooth. (I use a hand-held blender.)

Heat the oil in a saucepan, add the onion and sauté until golden brown. Add the blended ingredients and the chillies and cook, stirring often, until the masala has completely reduced and releases oil on the base of the pan. The more you fry this paste mixture, the deeper the resulting flavour, so it is a time-versus-flavour decision. Add the stock and bring to the boil, then add the meat and simmer for 4–5 minutes, or until cooked to your liking. Taste and add salt, ½ teaspoon freshly ground black pepper or more ground cardamom until you have a flavour you love, then serve.

SERVES 3–4

WITH LEMON
—

300 g Greek-style yoghurt

4–5 tablespoons sifted icing sugar

finely grated zest of 1 well-washed organic lemon

WITH LIME
—

300 g Greek-style yoghurt

4–5 tablespoons sifted icing sugar

finely grated zest of 1–2 well-washed limes

WITH ORANGE
—

300 g Greek-style yoghurt

4–5 tablespoons sifted icing sugar

finely grated zest of 1 well-washed organic orange

SIMPLE CITRUS YOGHURT DELUXE

Anna and Fanny Bergenström, *Under the Walnut Tree*

It doesn't get any easier than this! And the citrusy yoghurt is simply delectable on raspberries, blueberries or strawberries; or merely on its own, chilled in small glasses and served with almond biscotti or a wafer.

For lemon citrus yoghurt deluxe, combine the yoghurt with the icing sugar and the finely grated lemon zest.

For lime citrus yoghurt deluxe, combine the yoghurt with the icing sugar and the finely grated lime zest. Add extra icing sugar if needed, to taste.

For orange citrus yoghurt deluxe, combine the yoghurt with the icing sugar and the finely grated orange zest.

—

300 ml whipping cream

250 g mascarpone

grated zest and juice of
    2 lemons

100 g caster sugar

2 tablespoons maraschino
    liqueur, white wine
    or elderflower cordial

12 savoiardi biscuits (*sponge
    fingers*)

500 g strawberries

icing sugar for dusting

STRAWBERRY SAUCE

—

500 g strawberries

50–100 g caster sugar

QUICK STRAWBERRY AND LEMON TIRAMISU

Katie and Giancarlo Caldesi, *The Amalfi Coast*

This is a great quick dessert to make. Served in individual glasses it is very impressive to look at. We first tried it in Positano in a lovely restaurant called Next 2.

For the strawberry sauce, hull the strawberries and cut any large ones in half. Tip them into a large saucepan and add the sugar, according to the sweetness of the fruit. Bring to a gentle boil and cook for 15–20 minutes, or until the strawberries give easily when squished against the side of the pan. Strain through a sieve into a jug and when cool you can store the sauce covered in the refrigerator for up to 1 week.

In a bowl, whip the cream and then whisk in the mascarpone. Fold in the lemon zest and sugar, followed by the lemon juice. In a flat dish, mix the liqueur with 1½ tablespoons of the strawberry sauce, then dip the savoiardi biscuits into the liqueur until they are just soft but not soggy. Set aside six medium strawberries. Cut the remaining strawberries into slices. Lay the slices in the bottom of six martini glasses or tumblers so that the slices are facing outwards, then add a layer of cream, the remaining sauce and the soaked biscuits. Finish with a layer of cream. Decorate each glass with a fanned strawberry and lightly dust with icing sugar.

SERVES 4

—

125 g blueberries

1 cup frozen raspberries

3 tablespoons blanched almonds

2 tablespoons plain flour

¾ cup milk

75 g caster sugar

2 large eggs

1 tablespoon port or sherry

¼ teaspoon salt

20 g cold unsalted butter

icing sugar to dust (*optional*)

whipped cream to serve

BLUEBERRY AND RASPBERRY CLAFOUTIS

Margaret Fulton, *Baking*

This light dessert takes no time to put together, and it always impresses with its creamy silken texture and generous filling of berries.

Preheat the oven to 200°C. Butter a 6 cup gratin dish or other ovenproof dish. Tip the blueberries into the prepared dish and sprinkle the raspberries around.

In a blender or food processor, grind the almonds with the flour then add the milk, 4 tablespoons of the sugar, the eggs, the port or sherry and the salt, then blend the custard well. It will be necessary to stop the machine and scrape down the side once or twice. Pour the custard slowly over the fruit, dot with the butter and sprinkle with the remaining 2 tablespoons sugar. Bake the clafoutis in the middle of the preheated oven for 30–40 minutes or until the top is golden and the custard is set. Transfer it to a wire rack and let it cool for 20 minutes. Dust with icing sugar (if using) and serve the clafoutis warm with the whipped cream.

Vanessa Levis

ZABAGLIONE WITH BITTER CHOCOLATE SAUCE

Antonio Carluccio, *Simple Cooking*

This terrific dessert is easy to make, delicious warm or cold and can be either eaten as it is, accompanied by polenta biscuits, used as a filling for choux pastry or made into ice cream.

SERVES 6

—

6 organic egg yolks

120 g caster sugar

170 ml moscato passito di antelleria, marsala or madeira

CHOCOLATE SAUCE

—

200 g good-quality dark chocolate (*at least 70% cocoa solids*), broken into pieces

100 ml double cream

Put the egg yolks and sugar in a heatproof bowl (preferably a copper pan with a rounded base) and whisk for a few minutes to obtain a smooth and pure foam. Add the chosen dessert wine and mix well. Have ready a saucepan of simmering water, in which the bowl will fit, without the base touching the water.

Put the bowl in place in the pan and beat continuously over the simmering water until the mixture starts to thicken. Divide the mixture between six glasses and chill.

In the same way – in a bowl over a pan of hot water, base not touching the water – melt the chocolate carefully. Add the cream, and stir well until smooth. Spoon this on top of the zabaglione. You can eat this immediately or chill it again before serving.

NOTE

—

To turn the zabaglione into an ice cream, fold in 250 ml whipped double cream after cooking and cooling, place in an ice cream maker and churn according to the manufacturer's instructions. Alternatively, transfer to a shallow bowl and freeze for 1 hour or until it begins to solidify. Whisk well with a fork, then return to the freezer. Repeat this process three more times, then freeze until firm.

Alastair Hendy

PLANT-BASED FEAST

The recipes in this chapter are testimony to how exciting plant-based meals can be and another reminder, as if we needed one, that protein does not have to be the star of the show.

There are starters, from Stefano de Pieri's delectable porcini mushroom-flavoured custard spread on chargrilled Italian bread and Luke Nguyen's crisp silken tofu in lemongrass, to sensational mains like Greg and Lucy Malouf's seven-vegetable tagine.

The desserts showcase the beauty of fruit, from Gabriel Gaté's mandarin mousse with blackcurrant coulis to Mark Best's orange and polenta cake — one the Sydney chef has been making for 25 years.

SFORMATO OF PORCINI

Stefano de Pieri, *New Italian Food*

I am a big fan of soft *sformati*, which are a kind of Italian custard made with a béchamel sauce. Almost any vegetable can be turned into a *sformato*: mushrooms, zucchini, capsicum, eggplant – you name it. They are vegetarian and can be served cold as a starter or as a main course accompaniment. They save my life whenever vegetarians are in for dinner. Porcini are Italian dried mushrooms. They are expensive, but you only need to use a few. You could also use porcini oil, which has some merit if not allowed to get too old and oxidised. A few drops can increase flavour.

SERVES 6
—

100 g dried porcini mushrooms
200 g cultivated mushrooms
40 g butter
2 tablespoons olive oil
1 egg, lightly beaten
½ cup grated parmesan
salt and pepper
slices of chargrilled Italian
　　bread to serve

BÉCHAMEL SAUCE
—

150 g butter
100 g plain flour
1.5 litres milk
freshly grated nutmeg

For the béchamel sauce, melt the butter and mix it with the flour. Cook a little but without browning. Stir in the milk, bit by bit, mixing with a wooden spoon. Initially the mixture will be like a gluggy lump but as you add the milk it will break down more and more. Cook it gently for around 20 minutes or a little longer, taking care that it does not stick to the bottom of the pan. Add freshly grated nutmeg to taste. This recipe should yield a fairly soft sauce, which is what we want. If it is too thick add more milk or water. If you think you have some lumps in it, pass it through a fine sieve and everything will be all right.

Soak the porcini mushrooms in twice their volume of warm water for about 10 minutes to reconstitute them. Squeeze dry and combine with the cultivated mushrooms.

Heat the butter and oil in a frying pan and sauté the mushrooms. Cook until the liquid has reduced and then purée in a food processor.

Preheat the oven to 160°C.

Mix the mushrooms with the béchamel sauce, egg and parmesan, and season with salt and pepper.

Mix well and pour into six lightly greased ovenproof dariole moulds (which are available from many supermarkets) or ceramic soufflé ramekins.

Fold a tea towel and place it in the bottom of a deep baking tray. Arrange the dariole moulds in the tray and pour in enough warm water to come halfway up the sides of the moulds. Bake in the oven for about 35 minutes, or until set. The sformato should be fairly firm to the touch. Serve with the chargrilled bread.

Earl Carter

LEEK AND MUSHROOM FLATBREADS

SERVES 6–8

—

2 knobs butter
1 large leek, washed, halved and
    cut into rough 1 cm dice
250 g mushrooms, sliced,
    such as oyster or button
250 ml double cream
150 g parmesan, grated
salt
freshly ground black pepper
a piece flatbread or
    1 flour tortilla
50 g fresh white breadcrumbs

Mark Hix, *Mark Hix on Baking*

Preheat the oven to 220°C.

Melt the butter in a heavy-based saucepan, add the leek and mushrooms and gently cook for 3–4 minutes, covered, until the vegetables have softened without colouring. Add the cream and two-thirds of the parmesan, season and simmer until the cream has reduced and is just coating the leek and mushrooms.

Put the flatbread or tortilla onto a baking tray and spread the leek and mushroom mix over, then scatter over the breadcrumbs and the remaining parmesan. Bake in the oven for about 10–12 minutes until golden, then leave to cool a little. Cut into small squares and serve immediately.

PENNE WITH PUMPKIN AND WALNUT CREMA

SERVES 4

—

400 g pumpkin, chopped
    into large chunks
½ onion, sliced into wedges
2 garlic cloves, unpeeled
⅓ cup extra-virgin olive oil
sea salt
2 tablespoons orange juice
1 teaspoon finely grated
    orange zest
1 tablespoon white miso
100 g walnuts, roasted
    and chopped
100 g penne rigate
180 g broccoli florets
2 tablespoons basil leaves,
    thinly sliced
8 pitted green olives, sliced
freshly ground black pepper

Tony Chiodo, *Feel Good Food*

Here's my version of a creamy vegetable sauce – without the cream. The sauce is sweet and nutty all in one mouthful. I often use this sauce as a filling for bakes or lasagne. You can also fold the penne into the sauce and bake it in the oven to make pasta al forno.

Preheat the oven to 175°C. Place the pumpkin, onion and garlic in a baking dish. Drizzle with 3 tablespoons oil and sprinkle with some sea salt. Bake for about 45 minutes, or until the pumpkin is soft. Allow to cool, then remove the skin from the pumpkin and garlic.

Place the pumpkin, onion and garlic in a food processor with the orange juice and zest, miso, half the chopped walnuts and the remaining oil. Process to make a smooth purée. Add more orange juice for a thinner sauce. Season to taste.

Cook the pasta in a saucepan of salted boiling water for about 6 minutes, or until almost al dente. Add the broccoli florets to the boiling water with the penne and blanch for 2–3 minutes, or until tender. Drain the penne and broccoli and toss together with the pumpkin sauce.

Serve the penne with the basil, olives and the remaining walnuts scattered on top.

THAI EGGPLANT COCONUT CURRY

Peter Kuruvita, *My Feast*

You probably walk past these eggplants, which look like perfect green balls, in the vegetable section of the greengrocer or supermarket and wonder what you would do with them. Well here is an easy and tasty wholesome vegetarian dish that will please the fussiest herbivore. This curry is a childhood favourite. I rang my cousin to get the recipe and she gave me the following. As with most Sri Lankan curries, each household will make it slightly differently. This is the Dehiwala Kuruvita version.

SERVES 6
—
900 g Thai eggplants
50 ml vegetable oil
¼ teaspoon brown mustard seeds
½ onion, chopped
1 curry leaf sprig, leaves picked
1 garlic clove, chopped
1 small green chilli, chopped
2 teaspoons Sri Lankan
    curry powder
1 teaspoon ground turmeric
1 teaspoon Maldive fish flakes
300 ml water
250 ml coconut cream
juice of ½ lime
salt to taste

To prepare the eggplants, place them in a plastic bag and gently tap them until they all split open. Remove from the bag and pull out all the seeds and stems. Cut the eggplants into even strips, rinse in cold water and set aside.

Heat the oil in a heavy-based saucepan over medium heat, add the mustard seeds and cook until they start to pop. Add the onion and curry leaves and cook until the onion starts to turn brown.

Add the eggplant, garlic, chilli, curry powder, turmeric and fish flakes, and stir to combine. Add the water, bring to the boil, then reduce the heat to a simmer and cook for about 5 minutes or until the eggplant is soft.

Add the coconut cream and bring to the boil, then immediately remove from the heat. Finish with the lime juice and season with salt.

NOTE
—

Maldive fish flakes are Sri Lankan cuisine's equivalent to shrimp paste or fish sauce used in Thai, Indonesian or Malay cooking. Very strong in aroma and with a smoky flavour, they are an essential component to achieving an authentic Sri Lankan piquancy, and are added to most curries. You can buy them from Asian supermarkets or online.

CRISP SILKEN TOFU IN LEMONGRASS

Luke Nguyen, *The Food of Vietnam*

I learnt this recipe from a lady who also taught me how to make my own tofu. Her name is Mrs Ha, and she and her family have been making fresh tofu in Quy Nhon for five generations. Eating freshly made tofu is so different from eating tofu that has been packaged and sitting in a refrigerator for a week. If you ever get the chance to purchase freshly made tofu, please do so!

SERVES 4–6 AS PART OF A SHARED MEAL

—

450 g silken or firm tofu

1 lemongrass stem, white part only, finely chopped

1 red bird's eye chilli, finely chopped

1 tablespoon finely diced garlic

1 teaspoon sea salt

1 teaspoon sugar

½ teaspoon freshly ground black pepper

80 ml vegetable oil

coriander sprigs to garnish

sliced chilli to garnish

soy sauce to serve

jasmine rice to serve

Drain the tofu and cut into 5 x 10 cm chunks. Leave on the chopping board, or transfer to a tray.

In a bowl, combine the lemongrass, chilli, garlic, salt, sugar and pepper and mix together. Reserve half the spice mixture, and use the remainder to coat the tofu on both sides.

Heat a large frying pan over medium–high heat. Add the oil and fry the tofu for 3 minutes on each side, or until browned and crisp. Transfer to a serving plate.

Add the remaining spice mixture to the pan and cook for 1 minute, or until fragrant. Spoon the mixture over the tofu.

Garnish with the coriander and sliced chilli and serve with soy sauce and jasmine rice.

MISO-GLAZED EGGPLANT ᴡɪᴛʜ PICKLED GINGER ᴀɴᴅ SPRING ONION

Matt Wilkinson, *Mr Wilkinson's Simply Dressed Salads*

In 2007 I had this most memorable meal in Tokyo. We were greeted at the door by the manager, who asked if we spoke Japanese. Obviously not, but his words were, 'It's okay, I speak English!' He lied, but it turned out to be a fun-filled night of great food and lots of sake. I had a version of something like this dish, but grilled in a wood-fired oven and served with mashed foie gras.

SERVES 2–4
—

2 large eggplants, cut in half
    lengthways, then flesh
    scored all over
    in a crisscross pattern
canola oil (*non GM*), for brushing
30 ml mirin
2 tablespoons yellow miso paste
1 teaspoon caster sugar
1 teaspoon Japanese chilli flakes
    (*these are a bit finer than
    regular chilli flakes, but you
    can use the regular ones
    instead*)
2 teaspoons sesame seeds,
    half of them lightly toasted
    for garnishing
1 tablespoon white sesame oil
    (*please try to get white sesame
    oil for this dish, or use a good-
    quality regular sesame oil*)
1 teaspoon rice wine vinegar
2 spring onions, white and green
    bits separated, then thinly
    sliced
1 teaspoon pickled ginger
    (*from a jar*), finely chopped
300 g organic silken tofu,
    cut into 12 portions

Preheat the oven to 190°C. Place the eggplants on a large baking tray, skin side down, and brush with some canola oil. Cover the tray with foil and bake the eggplants for 40–60 minutes, or until a skewer can be inserted through them easily.

Remove from the oven and leave until cool enough to handle. Being careful not to break the skin, scoop out the eggplant flesh, into a bowl. Place the eggplant shells on the baking tray, on their backs, ready to hold the filling.

Break up the eggplant flesh by mixing through the mirin, miso paste, sugar, chilli flakes, untoasted sesame seeds, sesame oil, rice wine vinegar, white spring onion bits and pickled ginger. Gently fold in the tofu. Spoon the mixture into the eggplant shells and bake for a further 10 minutes, until all glazed.

Lay the filled eggplants on serving plates. Sprinkle with the toasted sesame seeds and green spring onion bits. Serve warm.

Jacqui Melville

SEVEN-VEGETABLE TAGINE

Greg and Lucy Malouf, *Malouf: New Middle Eastern Food*

This Moroccan classic makes a superb vegetarian main course, served with yoghurt cheese (labneh), onion jam and green harissa broth. Serve the green harissa broth in a separate jug, for each person to help themselves. If you have a couscoussier, stew the vegetables in the bottom section and steam the couscous on top. Otherwise you can use a steamer. The traditional method we have given here for the couscous is more time-consuming but gives a lighter, fluffier result.

SERVES 4

—

2 carrots
1 small butternut pumpkin
2 small turnips
2 small parsnips
1 small eggplant
1 zucchini
4 small waxy potatoes
1 tablespoon sweet paprika
½ tablespoon ground ginger
½ tablespoon crushed dried chillies
½ tablespoon ground cumin
½ tablespoon ground coriander
½ tablespoon freshly ground black pepper
seeds from 4 cardamom pods, crushed
1 garlic clove, crushed with ½ teaspoon salt
juice of 1 lemon
100 ml olive oil
500 ml vegetable stock
100 g chickpeas (*soaked in water to cover overnight, then drained and cooked until just tender*)
2 teaspoons rosewater

For the yoghurt cheese, mix the yoghurt with the salt. Spoon into a clean muslin square or a tea towel. Tie the four corners together and suspend the bundle from a wooden spoon over a deep bowl.

Put it in the refrigerator and allow it to drain for 24–72 hours. The longer the hanging time, the firmer the result.

For the onion jam, soak the currants in 50 ml of the dry sherry.

Melt the butter in a heavy-based pan, and slowly sweat the onions until they're soft and translucent, about 5 minutes. Add the remaining sherry and the port and continue to cook for a further 45 minutes over very low heat, stirring from time to time to ensure the jam doesn't stick to the bottom of the pan. Add the currants and the soaking liquor and cook for a further 10 minutes, or until the onions have become very sticky and almost caramelised. Season with salt and pepper. (The relish will keep, refrigerated, for up to 4 weeks.)

For the green harissa, which you need to make for the green harissa broth, seed and shred the large green chillies and remove the stalks from the spinach leaves.

Dry-fry the caraway and coriander seeds in a frying pan over medium heat until fragrant. Allow to cool.

Combine all the dry ingredients in a food processor, whiz for a minute, and then, with the machine still running, slowly add the olive oil until the mixture is the consistency of pouring cream. Season with sea salt and freshly ground black pepper. Pour into a jar, top with a thin layer of olive oil and refrigerate. (It will keep for about a week.)

YOGHURT CHEESE

—

1 kg Greek-style yoghurt
1 teaspoon sea salt
50 ml extra-virgin olive oil

ONION JAM

—

50 g currants
300 ml dry sherry
50 g unsalted butter
5 red onions, thinly sliced
250 ml tawny port

GREEN HARISSA

—

125 g large green chillies
100 g fresh spinach leaves
1 teaspoon caraway seeds
1 teaspoon coriander seeds
1 garlic clove
2 cups fresh coriander leaves
1 teaspoon dried mint
½ teaspoon chilli powder
60 ml olive oil
sea salt

COUSCOUS

—

250 g couscous
2 tablespoons olive oil
aromatics such as 1 cinnamon
    stick, ½ onion, grated lemon
    zest or a few thyme sprigs
5 g butter

GREEN HARISSA BROTH

—

2–3 tablespoons green harissa
    (see method), or to taste
400 ml vegetable stock
    or water, simmering
sea salt and freshly ground
    black pepper

For the couscous, sprinkle it into a shallow dish, add 250 ml cold water and let it sit for 10 minutes. Then rake it through with your fingers. Add 1 tablespoon of the olive oil and lightly season with sea salt and freshly ground black pepper.

Line a steamer or couscoussier with a damp cloth. Sit it on top of a saucepan boiling water flavoured with the aromatics. Tip the couscous into the top section, steam for 15 minutes, then pour it onto a tray. Fork it through lightly and allow it to cool for about 5 minutes. Sprinkle it with 4 tablespoons cold water and pour the remaining oil into your hands. Rub the couscous between the palms of your hands to break down any clumps into individual grains. This will take about 5 minutes. Put the couscous back into the cloth and steam it again for 20 minutes. Pour it out and fork the butter through it. Set aside and keep warm.

During the second steaming, begin to prepare the vegetables. Scrape the carrots and cut them into wedges diagonally. Peel the butternut pumpkin and cut it into 2 cm dice. Peel the turnips and cut them into wedges. Scrape the parsnips and cut them into batons. Cut the eggplant into wedges and cut the zucchini into wedges diagonally.

Boil the potatoes until tender, then remove the skins and cut them in half.

Preheat the oven to 200°C.

In a mixing bowl, combine all the spices with the garlic paste, lemon juice and half the olive oil.

Heat the remaining oil in a large flameproof, ovenproof casserole and sauté the carrots, pumpkin, turnips, parsnips and eggplant for about 5 minutes, or until all are lightly coloured. Add the spice mixture and stir to coat the vegetables for a further 2 minutes. Add the stock and cook for 5 minutes. Add the zucchini, chickpeas and potatoes. Mix them in well then place the casserole in the oven and bake for 20–30 minutes or until the vegetables are tender. Remove from the oven, check for seasoning and sprinkle the rosewater over the top.

When ready to serve, mix the green harissa into the simmering stock. Return to the boil, then taste and adjust the seasoning to your liking.

To serve the yoghurt cheese, tip it into a bowl and flatten the surface. Make a little well and fill with the extra-virgin olive oil.

Pile the vegetables into a deep serving dish and stack the couscous on top. Serve immediately with the onion jam, harissa broth and yoghurt cheese.

See photograph page 118.

MUSHROOM RAGU
WITH TRUFFLED POLENTA

Rosie Birkett, *A Lot on Her Plate*

This wow-factor meat-free supper is so easy to throw together. The dried mushrooms add an intense depth along with the broth you rehydrate them in. To make this totally vegetarian, use vegetable stock or water for the polenta, instead of chicken stock.

SERVES 2

—

15 g dried mushrooms (*porcini, chanterelle or Chinese*)

300 ml chicken stock

1 bay leaf

100 ml full-cream milk

80 g polenta

20 g mascarpone or butter

15 g parmesan, grated, plus extra to garnish

1 tablespoon truffle oil

1 tablespoon olive oil

1 garlic clove, finely chopped

3 French shallots, diced

knob butter

1–2 thyme sprigs

250 g mixed fresh mushrooms (*chestnut, shiitake, portobello, white*)

1 teaspoon finely chopped fresh tarragon or ¼ teaspoon dried tarragon

½ medium glass dry white wine

20 g flat-leaf parsley, finely chopped, leaves only, plus extra for garnish

a dash of tarragon vinegar or lemon juice

crème fraîche or mascarpone to serve (*optional*)

Put the dried mushrooms in a bowl and cover with 30 ml boiling water. Leave them to soak for 10–15 minutes while you prepare the polenta.

Put the chicken stock, a generous pinch of salt, the bay leaf and milk in a saucepan and bring to the boil. Once it's boiling, begin to gently whisk and slowly, steadily pour in the polenta until it's all combined. Turn the heat down to a simmer and cook, stirring with a wooden spoon occasionally, for 30 minutes, or until the polenta has absorbed all the liquid and is creamy and soft (if you're using quick-cook polenta, remove the pan from the heat 1 minute after you've stirred it in). If it's too thick and not wet enough, just add more water to loosen it – it should be the consistency of runny potato purée. Once cooked and thick and creamy, stir in the mascarpone (or butter), parmesan and truffle oil, and leave in a warm place until you're ready to serve.

For the mushroom ragu, heat the oil in a frying pan and add the garlic and shallots, stirring and cooking gently for about 4 minutes until soft and aromatic. Turn up the heat, add the butter and thyme, and start adding the fresh mushrooms, breaking up the bigger ones into the frying pan, coating them in the butter and garlic and shallot mixture. Season with sea salt and freshly ground black pepper and cook the mushrooms for 8–10 minutes until their juices start releasing and evaporating, and they are caramelising and crisping up slightly (to intensify their flavour). Depending on the size of your pan, you may need to do this in batches. When the mixture is fairly dry, add the tarragon, wine, rehydrated mushrooms and mushroom stock (passed through a fine sieve) and cook gently for 10 minutes. Transfer to a stainless steel bowl and check for seasoning, then add the parsley and a dash of vinegar or lemon juice for acidity.

Divide the warm polenta between two bowls and top with the mushroom ragu. Garnish with chopped parsley, parmesan, and if you like, some crème fraîche or mascarpone.

LEFT
Seven-vegetable tagine (recipe page 116)

DALI VEGETARIAN RICE NOODLE STIR-FRY

Luke Nguyen, *Luke Nguyen's Greater Mekong*

China invented noodles over 4000 years ago, and when I met the Zhao family in Dali I was in noodle heaven! They've been making rice noodles for four generations, but what makes theirs so unique is that they use a mixture of jasmine rice and white glutinous rice, giving the noodles a wonderful 'al dente' texture. Make the garlic water a day ahead and set aside. You can also make the yunnan chilli oil ahead of time (see method).

SERVES 4

—

2 tablespoons garlic water
   (*see method*)
2 tablespoons peanut oil
2 garlic cloves, finely chopped
90 g Chinese cabbage, sliced
120 g bean sprouts
8 garlic chives, cut into
   3 cm lengths
1 tablespoon light soy sauce
sea salt
250 g fresh round Chinese
   rice noodles
½ teaspoon Vietnamese pickled
   ground chillies
2 spring onions, sliced diagonally

YUNNAN CHILLI OIL

—

125 ml peanut oil
2 tablespoons chilli flakes
1 tablespoon sesame oil

To make garlic water, simply combine 1 tablespoon chopped garlic and 2 tablespoons water in a bowl. Cover and stand overnight, then strain.

You can make the yunnan chilli oil ahead of time. Heat the peanut oil in a wok until it almost reaches smoking point. Turn off the heat and allow the oil to cool for about 3 minutes. Place the chilli flakes in a glass jar, then pour in the hot oil, followed by the sesame oil. Allow to cool slightly before sealing; do not strain or discard the chilli. The oil will keep for up to a month stored in a cool, dark place and can be used in other noodle recipes.

Heat a wok or large frying pan until smoking. Add the peanut oil and sauté the garlic over medium–high heat until fragrant. Now add the cabbage, bean sprouts and garlic chives and stir-fry for 1 minute.

Add 1 teaspoon of the yunnan chilli oil, the soy sauce and a pinch of sea salt and stir-fry for a further minute. Next add the noodles, pickled ground chillies, garlic water and half the spring onion. Stir-fry for another 3 minutes. Transfer to a platter or individual plates, garnish with the remaining spring onion and serve.

NOTE

—

Vietnamese pickled ground chillies Known as *tuong ot* in Vietnamese, this table condiment and seasoning is made of fresh chillies, ground garlic, salt, sugar and vinegar. It is widely used in dressings, dipping sauces, soups, salads and stir-fries. It is sold in jars and very commonly available from Asian supermarkets.

Stuart Scott

MANDARIN MOUSSE WITH BLACKCURRANT COULIS

Gabriel Gaté, *100 Best Cakes and Desserts*

A lovely way to finish a fine dinner, this mousse is out of this world. Below are options for both blackcurrant and raspberry coulis – you can use either.

SERVES 6–8

—

100 g caster sugar
juice of 6 mandarins
juice of 1 lemon
finely grated zest of ½ lemon
10 g powdered gelatine
3 egg whites
pinch of cream of tartar
100 ml pouring cream,
    whipped until firm
icing sugar for dusting
mint leaves to serve *(optional)*

BLACKCURRANT COULIS

—

juice of 1 orange
juice of 1 lemon
80 g caster sugar
½ vanilla bean, split lengthways
300 g fresh or frozen
    blackcurrants

RASPBERRY COULIS

—

300 g raspberries
juice of 1 orange
juice of 1 lemon
2 tablespoons caster sugar

If making blackcurrant coulis, combine all the ingredients in a saucepan. Bring to a simmer, then cook for 5 minutes. Push the fruit through a fine sieve, then set aside to cool. Refrigerate until 10 minutes before serving.

If making raspberry coulis, in a food processor, blend all the ingredients to a purée. Strain the coulis to remove the seeds, then refrigerate until 10 minutes before required.

Place two-thirds of the sugar, the mandarin juice, lemon juice and lemon zest in a saucepan. Bring to a simmer and cook for about 5 minutes or until reduced by more than half.

Transfer the mandarin mixture to a heatproof bowl. Whisk in the gelatine until dissolved, then set aside to cool.

Using electric beaters, beat the egg whites and cream of tartar until stiff peaks form. Beat in the remaining sugar until combined.

Whisk the whipped cream into the mandarin mixture. Gently fold in the beaten egg whites until just combined.

Transfer the mousse to a large serving bowl or individual moulds or glasses. Refrigerate for at least 2–3 hours to set.

Serve the mousse with the coulis, dusted with icing sugar and garnished with mint leaves, if using. It is also lovely with fresh fruits.

ORANGE AND POLENTA CAKE

Mark Best, *Best Kitchen Basics*

Google pulled up 1,240,000 results for this cake in 22 seconds. I'm not sure when it became a thing but who knows what is going to go viral these days. The cake recipe is as sound as it is common and I've cooked it for 25 years. My version adds a kick with the syrup and Chartreuse chaser. Serve with crème fraîche or plain yoghurt.

SERVES 4

—

2 small oranges
butter for greasing
flour for dusting
5 large eggs (55 g)
170 g caster sugar
170 g ground almonds
50 g polenta
1 teaspoon baking powder

SYRUP

—

1 vanilla bean
230 g caster sugar
4 cardamom pods
2 star anise
50 ml Chartreuse

To make the syrup, split the vanilla bean and scrape the seeds into a small saucepan over medium–low heat – throw in the pod as well. Add the sugar, 250 ml water and the remaining spices. Bring to a gentle simmer, cook for 5 minutes then remove the pan from the heat. Add the Chartreuse and allow to infuse for 30 minutes. Strain into a clean container.

Put the oranges, unpeeled, in a saucepan, cover with water and bring to the boil over medium–high heat. Reduce the heat to medium–low, cover and simmer for 1¼ hours until the oranges are very soft. Drain and cool for 30 minutes.

Preheat the oven to 190°C. Butter a 24 cm springform cake tin and line the base with a disc of baking paper. Butter the tin again, including the paper, and lightly dust with flour – shake out any excess.

Coarsely chop the boiled oranges, removing any pips, then transfer them to a food processor and purée.

Whisk together the eggs and sugar for 2 minutes. Stir in the ground almonds and polenta and sift in the baking powder. Add the puréed oranges and mix well. Pour the mixture into the tin and bake for 40–45 minutes until light golden and just firm to the touch. Leave to cool in the tin for 10 minutes, then turn out onto a wire rack to cool.

Transfer the cake to a serving plate and use a skewer to prick it all over. Spoon over some of the syrup and allow it to soak in before adding more. Continue until all the syrup has been used.

VERBENA-SCENTED BREAD AND BUTTER PUDDING WITH PEACHES AND RASPBERRIES

Philippa Sibley, *New Classics*

This has become my family's Christmas pudding. As we celebrate Christmas in summer in Australia, when stone fruits and berries are in all their glory and panettone graces the shelves of the Mediterranean delis, I bring these together in a festive, warm but fresh, fruity pudding more suited to our climate. Lemon verbena thrives in summer and imparts a delightful flavour that has an affinity with peaches. I suggest you get your hands on a plant.

SERVES 6
—

250 ml milk

500 ml thickened cream,
    plus extra to serve

200 g egg yolks

1 whole egg

150 g caster sugar, plus extra
    for dusting

1 cup lemon verbena leaves,
    plus extra for garnish

5 perfectly ripe yellow peaches

soft butter for greasing

1 x 750 g plain panettone

500 g fresh raspberries

Preheat the oven to 150°C.

Bring the milk and cream to the boil. Stir the egg yolks and whole egg in a heatproof bowl then add the caster sugar. Add the hot cream mixture a little at a time, whisking continuously. Scrunch the lemon verbena leaves and add it to the mixture. Remove from the heat and allow to infuse for 10–15 minutes.

Bring a saucepan of water to the boil and have a bowl of iced water at hand. Split the peaches down the middle and remove the stones. Plunge the peach halves into the boiling water briefly, then drop into the iced water. Slip off their skins and slice each half into three wedges.

Butter a 2 litre capacity baking dish generously with soft butter, then dust with a little caster sugar. Slice the panettone and arrange in the dish. Disperse the peaches between the layers of panettone then strain over the custard mixture. Allow to soak for about 20 minutes, or until the panettone has soaked up the liquid and become quite squishy. Put the baking dish in the oven and cook for 30 minutes, or a little longer if the custard is still liquid.

To serve, scatter the raspberries and some additional lemon verbena leaves over the warm pudding and serve with some thickened cream on the side.

MANGO PANNA COTTA WITH WATERMELON, PINEAPPLE AND MINT SALSA

Luke Nguyen, *The Food of Vietnam*

This dessert showcases some of the amazing produce of the Mekong Delta region: plump mangoes, sweet pineapple, juicy watermelon, fresh mint, coconut and cashews. Jenny Pham, our chef at Red Lantern, incorporated this refreshing dish into our summer menu. It was a winner!

SERVES 4

—

1 ripe mango, weighing about
   500 g, peeled and diced
300 ml thickened cream
220 ml coconut cream
1½ tablespoons caster sugar
2 teaspoons powdered gelatine
unsalted crushed roasted
   cashews, to garnish

WATERMELON, PINEAPPLE AND MINT SALSA

—

100 g watermelon, seeds
   removed, flesh finely diced
100 g pineapple, peeled, core
   removed, flesh finely diced
1 tablespoon icing sugar
2 teaspoons lemon juice
10 mint leaves, thinly sliced

Put the mango flesh in a food processor and blend to a smooth purée. Set aside.

Place the cream, coconut cream and sugar in a small saucepan and stir over medium heat for 3 minutes, or until well combined and heated through.

Pour 2–3 tablespoons hot water into a small bowl and sprinkle the gelatine over. Whisk with a fork to dissolve the gelatine.

Stir the mango purée into the warm cream mixture, then strain through a fine sieve, into a jug. Add the gelatine mixture and stir well to combine.

Pour 185 ml of the panna cotta mixture into four glasses. Cover with plastic wrap and chill in the refrigerator for 4–6 hours, until set.

Near serving time, combine all the salsa ingredients and mix well. Serve each panna cotta topped with the salsa and a sprinkling of crushed cashews.

Alan Benson

ULTIMATE PICNIC

Michael Fountoulakis

Everybody loves a picnic but sometimes it can be a challenge to push the boat out beyond the predictable. This chapter presents a nice line-up of transportable treats to suit all budgets and time frames.

There are Asian flavours — Charmaine Solomon's Javanese-style fried meatballs, and Tracey Lister and Andreas Pohl's Vietnamese baguette with pâté and cold cuts — alongside traditionals with a twist, like Lyndey Milan's prosciutto-wrapped Scotch eggs.

For salad inspiration, look to Ian Thorpe's roasted pumpkin and hazelnut number or Brent Owens' freekeh with almonds and pomegranates. Easy-to-handle sweets include pecan fudge blondies from Leiths School of Food and Wine, Meyer lemon bars, and a banana bread Mark Best declares is best ever.

CHEESE PIES
FROM ALONISSOS

Rebecca Seal, *The Islands of Greece*

I first tried – far too many of – these dangerously tasty goat's cheese pies on one of my earliest trips to Greece, just after I finished university. I remember packing a little picnic of a few of them and some watermelon and hiring a boat down the coast to an inaccessible and deserted beach with black sand. There is a little friendly rivalry between the residents of Alonissos, a small and relatively unspoiled island in the Sporades group, and those of neighbouring Skopelos, as both believe they invented these delicacies.

MAKES 10

—

350 g soft, mild rindless
    goat's cheese, crumbled
10 filo pastry sheets,
    each measuring about
    20 cm square
flavourless vegetable oil
    for frying
olive oil for frying

Keep the remaining filo covered with a damp tea towel while you make each pie, as filo dries out and becomes brittle very fast.

Lay a pastry square out on a work surface. Scatter 35 g of the cheese over the pastry, avoiding the left- and right-hand edges by about 4 cm on each side. Working from the furthest edge of the pastry, turn the pastry down over the cheese, so it covers half the remaining pastry. Do the same with the bottom edge, so the cheese is completely covered. Pinch together both the right- and left-hand edges of the pastry and pull one end round to coil it into a spiral; be gentle or the pastry will rip. Repeat with the remaining pastry and cheese.

Pour about 5 mm each of the vegetable and olive oils into a wide frying pan with high sides placed over a high heat. When it is hot, reduce the heat to medium.

Using a wide spatula, slide the pastry spirals into the hot oil, in batches, being sure not to crowd the pan. If it looks as though any of them might unravel, place the loose end of the spiral against the edge of the frying pan; as soon as it starts to crisp up it will hold its shape. Fry for about 4 minutes or until the pastry is golden brown on the bottom. Using the spatula and a wooden spoon, very carefully flip the cheese pies over, being sure not to splash yourself with hot oil. Fry the other sides until golden brown all over and crisp on the edges. Remove from the hot oil and drain on paper towels. Keep warm while you cook the remaining pastries, adding more oil if necessary, bringing it up to temperature before adding the next batch of pies. Serve while hot.

Steven Joyce

QUICK HORSERADISH PINWHEELS

Philadelphia cream cheese
freshly grated horseradish
    (or store-bought prepared
    horseradish cream)
soft unleavened flatbread
wafer-thin slices of cold smoked
    salmon or smoked turkey
watercress or parsley to garnish

Anna and Fanny Bergenström, *Under the Walnut Tree*

Serve these nice little nibbles, either as finger food at a party or as part of a picnic basket.

Spread a soft mixture of room temperature Philadelphia cream cheese and some freshly grated horseradish (or store-bought prepared horseradish) on soft unleavened flatbread. Cover with a layer of wafer-thin slices of cold smoked salmon or smoked turkey. Roll tightly into thin rolls, wrap them in plastic wrap and chill for at least 1 hour.

Slice the rolls into 3 cm thick pinwheels and arrange on a serving platter garnished with a bit of watercress or parsley.

ROASTED PUMPKIN AND HAZELNUT SALAD

SERVES 4–6

—

800 g pumpkin, peeled and
    cut into 2 cm cubes
1 red onion, quartered
2 tablespoons olive oil
sea salt
freshly ground black pepper
1 tablespoon lemon juice
200 g baby spinach leaves
¼ cup hazelnuts, roasted
    and roughly chopped

Ian Thorpe, *Eat Well Now*

This is a really no-fuss, simple salad – something you can turn to when you're having an everyone's-here-in-an-hour-and-I-haven't-started-cooking emergency. I make it once a week and usually grill some chicken or fish or sometimes beef to have with it. You could also scatter it with some fresh goat's cheese for a good picnic dish or light lunch. My favourite types of pumpkin to use are butternut or blue.

Preheat the oven to 220°C. Put the pumpkin and onion in a large baking dish and drizzle with 1 tablespoon of the oil. Season with salt and pepper and toss well. Roast for 40 minutes or until golden brown, then leave to cool to warm or to room temperature, depending on your preference. (In winter I like to serve the salad warm, while in summer I serve it cool.)

Meanwhile, make the dressing by combining the remaining oil with the lemon juice in a small bowl.

Tip the roasted pumpkin and onion into a large bowl and add the spinach, hazelnuts and dressing. Toss to combine, and serve.

—

165 g cracked freekeh, rinsed

500 ml vegetable stock or water

½ teaspoon cumin seeds

a few drops of rosewater

2 spring onions, thinly sliced

seeds of 1 pomegranate

60 g slivered almonds

½ teaspoon sumac

1 long red chilli, finely diced

1 bunch flat-leaf parsley leaves,
    finely chopped

1 bunch mint leaves, torn

1 garlic clove, crushed

60 ml olive oil

juice of 2 lemons

FREEKEH SALAD WITH ALMONDS AND POMEGRANATES

Brent Owens, *Dig In!*

Freekeh is a superfood that's high in fibre, cheap and very easy to cook and it's available at the supermarket. It can be used in salads or tossed with some vegetables for dinner. If you use uncracked freekeh, you will need to increase the cooking time to around 50 minutes.

Put the freekeh, stock, cumin seeds and rosewater in a large saucepan over high heat. Bring to the boil then reduce the heat to medium–low and cook, covered, until the liquid has been absorbed and the freekeh is just tender, about 20 minutes.

Tip the freekeh out onto a tray and spread it in an even layer to cool.

Combine all the ingredients in a bowl and season with salt and pepper. Check for seasoning and whether there is enough acidity from the lemon – it should be slightly tangy. Adjust as necessary and serve.

MAKES: ABOUT
60–70 MEATBALLS

—

500 g minced beef

2 onions, finely chopped

2 garlic cloves, crushed with
    1 teaspoon salt

2 fresh red chillies, seeded
    and finely chopped or
    1 teaspoon sambal oelek

500 g floury potatoes,
    boiled and mashed

2 teaspoons chopped dark
    palm sugar

½ teaspoon dried shrimp paste

1 tablespoon dark soy sauce

1 tablespoon lemon juice

3 teaspoons ground coriander

2 teaspoons ground cumin

1 teaspoon freshly grated
    nutmeg or ground mace

1 egg, beaten

peanut oil for deep-frying

JAVANESE-STYLE FRIED MEATBALLS

Charmaine Solomon, *The Complete Asian Cookbook*

Freely adopted from Dutch frikkadels, with hot chillies and spices giving a local flavour, these meatballs, locally known in Indonesia as *pergedel goreng jawa*, can be served hot as a snack or cold as picnic fare.

Put the beef into a large bowl. Add the onion, garlic, chilli and mashed potato and use your hands to combine.

In a small bowl, dissolve the palm sugar and shrimp paste in the combined soy sauce and lemon juice, then stir in the coriander, cumin and nutmeg. Add to the minced meat with the egg and continue to mix all the ingredients together until well combined. Take small portions of the mixture at a time and shape into small balls. Cover and refrigerate for at least 1 hour.

Heat the peanut oil in a wok or large heavy-based saucepan over medium heat. When the oil is hot, deep-fry the balls, in batches, for 3–4 minutes, turning regularly, until brown on all sides and cooked through. Drain on paper towel and serve.

BAGUETTE WITH PÂTÉ AND COLD CUTS

Tracey Lister and Andreas Pohl, *Vietnamese Street Food*

We particularly like roast pork or char siu, which can be purchased at Asian grocery stores or butchers, as fillings. Alternatively, ham or poached chicken are also good. Fried tofu can be added for some extra crunch.

SERVES 6

—

6 small baguettes
120 g mayonnaise
180 g pâté
12 slices of your favourite
    cooked meat
3 long chillies, thinly sliced
60 g coriander sprigs
3 cucumbers, peeled and sliced
200 g carrot and daikon pickle
    (*see below*)
1½ tablespoons classic dipping
    sauce (*see below*)

CARROT AND DAIKON PICKLE

—

250 g carrots
200 g daikon
200 ml rice vinegar
110 g sugar
2 teaspoons salt

CLASSIC DIPPING SAUCE

—

60 ml fish sauce
100 ml lime juice
1 teasooon rice vinegar
110 g sugar
2 garlic cloves, finely chopped
1 long red chilli, finely chopped

For the carrot and daikon pickle, peel the carrots and daikon, cut into 5 cm batons and place in a jar with a lid.

To make the pickling liquid, combine the vinegar, sugar, salt and 250 ml water in a small saucepan. Heat until the sugar has completely dissolved, then cool until lukewarm.

Pour the pickling liquid over the vegetables and leave for at least 1 hour before serving. (Store in the refrigerator for up to 2 weeks.)

For the classic dipping sauce, combine the fish sauce, lime juice, rice vinegar and sugar in a small bowl. Stir until the sugar has completely dissolved.

Add the garlic and chilli and serve in dipping bowls.

Preheat the oven to 180°C. Heat the baguettes in the oven for 1 minute, then cut in half lengthways and remove some of the soft centre.

Spread the mayonnaise on the top half of each baguette and the pâté on the bottom half. Fill the centre with the cooked meat, chilli, coriander, cucumber and pickle.

Drizzle the dipping sauce over the baguette filling.

PROSCIUTTO-WRAPPED SCOTCH EGGS

Lyndey Milan, *Lyndey Milan's Taste of Australia*

Amanda Walker, one of the hosts on the F.O.O.D (Food of Orange District) train in New South Wales, made these with a clever technique for baking them rather than deep-frying. I prefer using prosciutto to bacon but, either way, these eggs are perfect for a picnic breakfast or anytime.

MAKES 12

—

13 free-range eggs
5 slices white bread,
    crusts removed
200 ml milk
500 g minced pork
500 g minced veal
2 tablespoons finely chopped
    flat-leaf parsley
1 tablespoon thyme leaves
½ teaspoon freshly grated
    nutmeg
salt and freshly ground black
    pepper
12 prosciutto slices or very
    thin bacon rashers
rocket to serve
tomato chutney to serve

Preheat the oven to 170°C. Lightly oil 12 holes (170 ml capacity) in a large-sized muffin tin.

Place 12 of the eggs into a saucepan of hot water and bring to the boil. Stir to ensure the egg yolks will centre in the whites. Simmer for 5 minutes from the time the water starts to bubble. Drain the eggs and run under cold water until cool. Peel carefully.

Soak the bread in the milk for 1 minute. Drain and squeeze dry. Place the bread and minces into a large bowl and use your hands to combine. Then add the remaining egg, the parsley, thyme and nutmeg and season with salt and pepper. Mix to combine evenly and divide into 12 balls.

Press the mince mixture firmly around each boiled egg, ensuring the entire egg is covered. Then wrap a piece of prosciutto around the middle of each egg and place them into the prepared muffin tin.

Bake for 25 minutes until nicely browned. Allow to cool for a few minutes before draining on paper towel. Serve halved, warm or cold, with rocket and tomato chutney.

Stuart Scott

RASPBERRY MACARONS
WITH WHITE CHOCOLATE

Bitesize: Macarons, Cake Pops and Cute Things

After the incredible popularity of the macaron, they are now finding their way into picnic hampers all over the world. This is a particularly delicious recipe, with its combination of pink raspberry macarons filled with white chocolate ganache. They'd bring an elegance to any picnic and would be perfect with a glass of pink champagne.

MAKES 30
—

20 g ground almonds
220 g icing sugar
110 g egg whites
30 g caster sugar
2 teaspoons natural raspberry extract
pink food colouring (*paste or powdered is preferable*)

WHITE CHOCOLATE GANACHE
—

120 g white chocolate, chopped
2½ tablespoons pouring cream
2 teaspoons natural raspberry extract
3 teaspoons raspberry jam

Line two baking trays with baking paper. Process the ground almonds and icing sugar in a food processor until combined, then sift twice. Place the egg white in the bowl of an electric mixer and beat on medium speed until frothy, then increase the speed while gradually adding the caster sugar. Continue beating until stiff peaks form, then mix in the raspberry extract and enough colouring for desired effect. Fold one-third into the almond mixture and combine well. Gently fold through the remaining eggwhite mixture; it should be glossy and thick, not thin and runny.

Transfer to a piping bag fitted with a 5 mm plain nozzle and pipe 3 cm circles about 3 cm apart onto the trays. Leave at room temperature for 1–6 hours (depending on the humidity) or until a crust forms; the macarons should no longer be sticky to the touch.

Preheat the oven to 140°C. Bake the macarons for 15–18 minutes until they rise slightly. Immediately slide the macarons and baking paper off the trays and onto wire racks to cool completely.

Meanwhile, to make the ganache, place the chocolate and cream in the top of a double boiler over medium heat and stir until melted and smooth. Refrigerate for 25–35 minutes or until firm but pliable. Add the raspberry extract and jam and mix well.

Transfer to a small piping bag fitted with a 1 cm plain nozzle and pipe about 1 teaspoon onto half of the macarons. Sandwich with the remaining macarons.

BEST EVER
BANANA BREAD

Mark Best, *Best Kitchen Basics*

Was there ever anything so pungently disappointing than a poor report and the forgotten locker banana at the end of school term? The world is broken down into simple sub-sets – those who like ripe bananas and those who don't. I'm with the latter. The dull grey shuffle of office life is surely not helped by the colon-blocking banality of commercial banana bread. This is something to do with bananas when the yellow starts to turn black. Cook and set yourself free.

MAKES 1 LOAF
—

250 g unsalted butter, cut into
   1 cm cubes and softened
335 g raw sugar
4 eggs, at room temperature
1 cinnamon stick
1 star anise
2 cloves
3 cardamom pods
½ teaspoon white peppercorns
300 g plain flour
3 teaspoons baking powder
6 ripe bananas
butter to serve (*optional*)

Preheat the oven to 160°C. Grease a 21 x 6 x 1 cm loaf tin with butter and neatly line it with baking paper.

In the bowl of a stand mixer fitted with the paddle attachment, cream the butter and sugar on high speed. Add the eggs, one at a time, scraping down the side of the bowl after each addition.

In an electric spice grinder, or using a mortar and pestle, process the spices to a fine powder.

Sift the spices into a bowl with the flour and baking powder.

Peel and coarsely chop the bananas and toss them through the spiced flour mixture to coat.

Gently fold the flour and banana into the creamed butter and sugar until fully incorporated.

Pour the mixture into the prepared tin and tap once firmly on a work surface to remove any air pockets. Bake for 45–50 minutes or until a thermometer inserted in the centre reads 85°C.

Allow to cool in the tin for 5 minutes before turning out onto a wire rack to cool completely.

Serve in slices with lashings of home-made or salted butter, if desired.

PECAN FUDGE BLONDIES

MAKES 18

—

150 g pecan nuts
140 g vanilla fudge
3 eggs, at room temperature
170 g unsalted butter, softened
75 g caster sugar
150 g soft light brown sugar
½ teaspoon natural vanilla
    extract
200 g plain flour
1 teaspoon baking powder
pinch of salt

Leiths School of Food and Wine, *How to Cook Cakes*

Classic blondies have a fudge-like flavour, achieved here with the brown sugar and vanilla combination as well as the pieces of actual fudge stirred in. These have the great flavour of pecan pie without the need for pastry making!

Heat the oven to 180°C. Line a shallow 32 x 30 cm baking tin with baking paper. Spread the pecan nuts out on a separate baking tray and toast in the oven for 10–15 minutes. Tip them onto a plate to cool, then roughly chop the nuts.

Cut the fudge into very small dice. Break the eggs into a small bowl and, using a fork, beat lightly to break them up. Set aside.

Cream the butter and sugars together in a medium bowl until pale and fluffy, using an electric whisk. Add the eggs in several additions, beating well after each addition, then stir in the vanilla, using a large metal spoon or a spatula. Sift in the flour, baking powder and salt and add the chopped pecans and all but 1 tablespoon of the fudge. Stir well to combine. Spoon the mixture into the prepared tin and scatter the remaining fudge over the surface. Bake in the middle of the oven for about 30 minutes until a skewer inserted into the centre comes out clean, or with a few moist crumbs still clinging to it. Remove from the oven and leave to cool in the tin set on a wire rack. Remove when almost cooled and peel away the lining paper. Cut into squares while still warm.

MEYER LEMON BARS

MAKES 24

—

6 eggs
550 g caster sugar
75 g plain flour
250 ml meyer lemon juice,
    strained
3 tablespoons finely grated
    meyer lemon zest

SWEET CRUST

—

225 g plain flour
65 g icing sugar, plus extra for
    dusting
180 g unsalted butter, cut into
    10 pieces

Bitesize: Macarons, Cake Pops and Cute Things

Preheat the oven to 180°C. To make the crust, place the flour and sugar in the bowl of a food processor and pulse to combine. Add the butter, 1 piece at a time, until the mixture resembles pea-sized crumbs. Press the mixture into the base of a 33.5 x 23.5 cm slice tin. Bake for 18–20 minutes or until golden. Cool in the tin for 20–30 minutes.

Reduce the temperature to 150°C. Whisk the eggs, sugar, flour and lemon juice together in a bowl until combined and smooth. Stir in the zest and pour over the crust. Bake for 25–30 minutes or until set. Remove from the oven and cool completely on a wire rack. Dust with the extra icing sugar and cut into 6 cm x 2.5 cm bars.

NOTE

—

Meyer lemons are available during the cooler months from select greengrocers and farmers' markets.

Marina Oliphant

DRINKS PARTY CANAPÉS

The best canapés are mouthfuls of deliciousness created from inventive combinations of ingredients. They leave you wanting more and perhaps even losing track of the conversation as you keep one eye on the second plate doing the rounds.

These recipes are an opportunity to present guests at your next drinks party with that very conundrum. Euro-inspired morsels include Laura Cassai's Tuscan chestnut pancakes topped with crispy pancetta, and Margaret Fulton's incomparable piroshki, alongside the Asian flavours of Leanne Kitchen and Antony Suvalko's coconut fish cakes with cucumber pickles.

Daniella Germain's fried banana chips are a friend for beer, and Tom Hunt's pulled pork, kale and kohlrabi kimchi creations lift the bar on the ubiquitous slider.

—

2 teaspoons salt

2 teaspoons chilli powder

4 plantains

125 ml vegetable oil for frying

FRIED BANANA CHIPS

Daniella Germain, *My Abuelo's Mexican Feast*

Plátanos fritos are moreish chips made from plantain, a type of large banana that is cooked when green to achieve a delicious flavour. These snacks are great with a cold beer on a hot day. Plantains are available from some greengrocers. If you can't find them, just use unripe bananas.

Place the salt and chilli powder in a glass jar with a lid. Close the jar and shake until the mixture is combined.

Peel the plantains and slice them lengthways into 5 mm thick slices.

Heat the vegetable oil in a deep frying pan over high heat. Fry 4–5 slices at a time for a few minutes or until just golden. Drain on paper towel.

Sprinkle with the salt–chilli mixture and serve immediately.

MAKES 24

—

1 small red capsicum

1 tablespoon chopped flat-leaf
   parsley

1 tablespoon lemon juice

350 g zucchini

250 g haloumi, grated

3 spring onions, chopped

75 g plain flour

2 eggs, lightly beaten

1 tablespoon chopped dill

sea salt and freshly ground
   black pepper

olive oil for shallow-frying

ZUCCHINI AND HALOUMI FRITTERS WITH ROASTED CAPSICUM SALSA

Bitesize: Tartlets, Quichettes and Cute Things

Preheat the oven to 180°C. Place the capsicum on a baking tray and roast for 20 minutes or until the skin has blackened. Transfer to a bowl, cover with plastic wrap and leave for 10 minutes. Remove the skin and seeds. Cut the capsicum into thin strips and place in a bowl with the parsley and lemon juice. Set aside until required.

Coarsely grate the zucchini. Wrap in a tea towel and wring out to remove excess moisture. Place in a bowl, add the haloumi, spring onion, flour, eggs and dill, season with salt and pepper and stir to combine.

Heat 2 cm oil in a large, heavy-based frying pan over medium heat, add 1 tablespoon amounts of the zucchini mixture, flatten out slightly and cook for 1–2 minutes on each side or until golden. Drain on paper towel and keep warm. Repeat with the remaining mixture. To serve, top each fritter with a spoonful of capsicum salsa.

Marina Oliphant

250 g shredded parmesan
1 celeriac
2 teaspoons dijon mustard
2 tablespoons lemon juice
60–100 ml pouring cream
sea salt and freshly ground black
     pepper
8 slices rare roast beef, halved
snipped chives for garnish

PARMESAN WAFERS WITH CELERIAC REMOULADE AND ROAST BEEF

Bitesize: Tartlets, Quichettes and Cute Things

These look elegant and quite complex, but really they are super-simple to put together. Just make sure you use really lovely, thinly sliced, rare beef.

Preheat the oven to 180°C. Line two baking trays with baking paper. Place 1 tablespoon amounts of parmesan on the trays, leaving 5 cm between them to allow for spreading. Bake for 8–10 minutes or until golden. Leave to cool on the trays.

Peel the celeriac and coarsely grate into a bowl. Add the mustard, lemon juice and enough cream to bring the mixture together. Season with salt and pepper.

To serve, top each wafer with a spoonful of the remoulade, half a slice of roast beef and garnish with the chives.

MAKES 30
—

200 g chestnut flour
sea salt flakes
extra-virgin olive oil for greasing
10 thin slices pancetta
150 g fresh ricotta

TUSCAN CHESTNUT SAVOURY PANCAKES

Laura Cassai, *My Italian Kitchen*

Necci are one of the simplest, yet most magical treats I have ever tasted. The first time I had *necci*, I was six years old. I was living in Tuscany, where this regional recipe comes from, and I can vividly remember the delicious aftertaste it left in my mouth. With the soft pillow of an ever-so-light chestnut pancake, creamy ricotta and crunchy pancetta, it's a dish that truly captures the essence of the most traditional Italian food.

Whisk the chestnut flour with 300 ml water and a pinch of sea salt in a bowl. Mix until you have a smooth batter.

Lightly grease a non-stick frying pan with olive oil and set over medium–high heat.

Place 1 tablespoon of batter in the pan for each mini pancake and cook for a couple of minutes, then flip and cook until golden brown. Set aside and keep warm.

Toss the pancetta slices in a frying pan over high heat until crispy. This should take no more than 5 minutes. Drain on paper towel.

To assemble, place the mini necci on a platter. Spoon on about 1 tablespoon ricotta and top with crunchy pancetta.

To serve as sweet pancakes, top with honey instead of pancetta.

Pictured page 7

PULLED PORK ⏤ AND ⏤ KALE ⏤ AND ⏤
KOHLRABI KIMCHI SLIDERS

Tom Hunt, *The Natural Cook*

Home-made kimchi is wonderful, with the added bonus of containing probiotics from the fermentation process (it won't contain these if you don't let it ferment). It is full of good bacteria that help keep your immune system healthy. The Koreans commonly use cabbage to make kimchi, so feel free to substitute that if you prefer. The kale and kohlrabi kimchi here makes about 1 kg, so you can either make a lot of sliders or have some left over. You will need to make the kimchi at least 2 days ahead of time.

—

left-over roast pork
warmed burger buns (*any size*)

KALE AND KOHLRABI
KIMCHI

—

1 quantity raw kale with sesame
    seeds and honey (*see below
    and method*)
4 tablespoons rice flour
8 garlic cloves
1 onion, roughly chopped
50 ml fish sauce
4 tablespoons Korean chilli
    powder or 2 tablespoons
    cayenne pepper
1 small kohlrabi, peeled and cut
    into 5 mm matchsticks
1 carrot, cut into 5 mm
    matchsticks
1 leek, thinly sliced
sesame seeds, to serve (*optional*)

RAW KALE WITH SESAME
SEEDS AND HONEY

—

400 g kale
juice of ½ lemon
1 tablespoon raw local honey
2–3 cm piece fresh ginger
2 tablespoons sesame seeds
extra-virgin olive oil (*optional*)

For the raw kale with sesame seeds and honey, pull the kale leaves off the thick stalks. Finely chop the stalks and roughly chop the leaves, then wash both. Drain well, then place in a bowl with 1 tablespoon salt, the lemon juice and honey. Massage the dressing into the leaves for 2–3 minutes, bruising them so they soak up the juices. Leave for 30 minutes, then pour off the excess liquid. Finely chop the ginger and add it to the kale with the sesame seeds. Mix and dress with extra-virgin oil, if you like.

For the kale and kohlrabi kimchi, bring 400 ml water to a gentle simmer with the rice flour. Keep stirring for a few minutes until it thickens and starts to bubble. Simmer for another 1–2 minutes until it becomes an opaque porridge.

Blend the garlic, onion and fish sauce in a blender or food processor to a purée. Transfer to a bowl, add the flour mixture and chilli powder and mix. Then add the kohlrabi, carrot and leek and finally the raw kale with sesame seeds and honey. Mix well.

Put into a sterilised non-metallic tub, such as a Tupperware box, and press down to pack it in. Put the lid on. Eat it fresh with sesame seeds sprinkled on top, or leave it at cool room temperature for 2–3 days. After 2 days, check if you can see any tiny bubbles; they will prove it is fermenting. If not, leave it out of the refrigerator a little longer, until the fermentation process starts. (Keep the kimchi in a sealed, non-metallic container in the refrigerator and eat within 3 weeks.)

Shred the roast pork using two forks and reheat it in a frying pan until hot right through. Serve in the warmed burger buns with a spoon of kimchi on top.

COCONUT FISH CAKES
WITH CUCUMBER PICKLES

Leanne Kitchen and Antony Suvalko, *East*

These Javanese-style fish cakes are simple to prepare, easy to cook and packed with flavour. Any white-fleshed fish will work and, while we've gone for snapper, by all means substitute with what's freshest, sustainable and well priced at your fishmonger or supermarket. No chilli required here – just whip up a batch of cucumber pickles and you're away!

MAKES ABOUT 25

—

4 small red Asian shallots, chopped

2 garlic cloves, chopped

2 candlenuts (*see note on page 77*), chopped

1.5 cm piece fresh galangal, chopped

1 cm piece fresh ginger, chopped

800 g boneless, skinless snapper, john dory or any other white-fleshed fish fillets, cut into 5 cm pieces

1½ teaspoons caster sugar

200 g fresh grated or thawed frozen grated coconut

2 eggs, lightly beaten

150 ml coconut milk

vegetable oil for deep-frying

CUCUMBER PICKLES

—

60 ml clear rice vinegar

2 tablespoons boiling water

55 g caster sugar

2 red bird's eye chillies, chopped

1 telegraph cucumber, peeled and halved lengthways

For the cucumber pickles, combine the rice vinegar, boiling water and sugar in a bowl and stir until the sugar has dissolved. Cool. Add the chopped chilli.

Remove the seeds from the cucumber using a teaspoon, then thinly slice the cucumber diagonally. Add to the vinegar mixture and stand for 1 hour before serving. Cucumber pickles are best served on the day they are made.

Combine the shallots, garlic, candlenuts, galangal and ginger in a food processor and process until a paste forms. Alternatively, use a mortar and pestle. Add the fish fillets and process until the mixture is smooth.

Transfer to a bowl and add the remaining ingredients, except the oil and pickles, and season to taste with salt and freshly ground black pepper.

Heat enough oil for deep-frying in a large wok until it reaches 170°C, or until a cube of bread turns golden in 20 seconds.

Using your hands, form 2 tablespoonfuls of the mixture into balls then flatten into thick discs about 5–6 cm across.

Fry the fish cakes, in batches, for about 12 minutes, turning once, or until deep golden and cooked through. Take care when cooking as the cakes are delicate. Transfer to a plate lined with paper towel to drain any excess oil then serve them hot with the cucumber pickles.

BABY CARAMELISED ONIONS TARTES TATIN

Bitesize: Tartlets, Quichettes and Cute Things

We all know how delicious traditional apple tartes tatin is, so why not create a mini savoury version using onions, which contain natural sugars that caramelise as beautifully as apples.

MAKES 20

—

80 ml olive oil

3 onions, thinly sliced

2 thyme sprigs, plus extra leaves
     for garnish

sea salt and freshly ground
     black pepper

50 g grated cheddar cheese

DOUGH

250 g self-raising flour

1 teaspoon salt

100 ml milk

40 g butter, melted

1 teaspoon dijon mustard

1 egg

Place the oil, onion and thyme in a frying pan over low heat and cook, stirring regularly, for 20–30 minutes or until softened and caramelised. Discard the thyme sprigs. Season with salt and pepper.

Preheat the oven to 180°C. Lightly grease two 12-hole mini-muffin tins.

Meanwhile, for the dough, sift the flour and salt into a bowl and make a well in the centre. Whisk the milk, butter, mustard and egg together in a separate bowl. Add to the dry ingredients and mix with a fork until the dough just comes together. Knead briefly on a floured work surface until smooth. Roll out to 1 cm thick and, using a 2.5 cm round cutter, cut into 20 circles.

Place a spoonful of onion in the base of each mini-muffin hole, sprinkle with some cheese and top with a circle of dough. Bake for 10–15 minutes or until golden. Leave in tins for 3–4 minutes. To remove the tartes, cover each tray with a large plate and invert the tartes onto the plate. Garnish with the extra thyme leaves.

LITTLE LAMB PIES WITH YOGHURT CHEESE AND POMEGRANATE

Greg and Lucy Malouf, *Malouf: New Middle Eastern Food*

These little pies from Baalbeck, known as *sfiha*, are renowned across Lebanon. Don't buy minced lamb from the supermarket for this recipe as it's far too fatty. You don't want the lamb to be too lean, however. Ask the butcher for lamb leg with some fat, but no sinews.

MAKES 12

—

DOUGH

310 g baker's flour
½ teaspoon salt
¾ teaspoon sugar
1 tablespoon dried yeast
50 ml warm water
150 g plain yoghurt
60 ml extra-virgin olive oil,
    plus extra to serve
pomegranate molasses to serve
Yoghurt cheese to serve
    (*see pages 116–17*)

MINCED LAMB MANOUSHI

—

250 g minced lamb
1 tomato, seeded and finely
    diced
1 small red onion, finely diced
⅓ cup finely shredded flat-leaf
    parsley leaves
1 teaspoon ground allspice
1 red bullet chilli, seeded and
    finely diced
1 teaspoon pomegranate
    molasses

For the minced lamb manoushi, place the minced lamb on a large chopping board and put the remaining ingredients on top. Use a large knife to chop and mix everything together until well combined. It should be the consistency of a fine paste. Season with sea salt and freshly ground black pepper. Set aside.

For the dough, sift the flour into a large mixing bowl and add the salt. Dissolve the sugar and yeast in the warm water in a small bowl. In another small bowl, whisk together the yoghurt and olive oil. Pour the bubbling yeast into the flour with the yoghurt mixture. Knead for about 10 minutes, until the dough is smooth and silky. Lightly oil the ball of dough and put it into a clean bowl. Cover and leave in a warm place to rise for 2 hours, by which time it should have at least doubled in size.

Preheat the oven to 200°C. Knock back the dough then tip it out onto a floured work surface.

Dust a rolling pin with flour, then roll the pastry out as thinly as you can. Cut it into 12 rounds, each about 10 cm in diameter. Place a spoonful of minced lamb mixture in the centre of each round. Moisten the edges of the pastry with a little water, then pinch the corners together to form the traditional shape.

Bake the pies for 8–10 minutes. Serve with a big dollop of yoghurt cheese, a drizzle of oil and a splash of pomegranate molasses.

DEEP-FRIED OYSTERS
WITH TONKATSU

Izakaya

SERVES 4

—

12 oysters, on the shell
60 g cornflour
2 eggs, lightly beaten
30 g panko (*Japanese
   breadcrumbs*)
oil for frying
tonkatsu sauce to serve
lemon wedges to serve

Slip the oysters from their shells and place on two layers of paper towel for 5 minutes before cooking. Rinse and dry the shells, then set aside.

Put the cornflour, eggs and panko in three separate bowls. Working one at a time, toss each oyster in the cornflour, dip in the egg, then roll in the panko to coat all over.

Pour in enough oil to reach 2 cm up the side of a frying pan and place over high heat. When the surface of the oil is shimmering, add the oysters and cook for about 30 seconds, or until golden.

Drain on paper towel, then return the oysters to their shells. Serve with the tonkatsu sauce and lemon wedges on the side.

PIROSHKI

Margaret Fulton, *Margaret Fulton Favourites*

I learnt about this recipe for soft buns filled with onion and smoked bacon in the 1970s from a Russian reader of *Woman's Day*, when we were running a national bake-off. In those days the recipe seemed so exotic and different – sausage rolls being our closest equivalent. I'd never tasted anything so good and have been making them ever since. We, the judges, were so impressed that we awarded the piroshki a major prize. I have since found out that there are many variations to these Russian meat pies — they may contain mince or cabbage, and are often fried instead of baked – but this is still the recipe I like the best. Piroshki also freeze well and, once thawed, need just 20 minutes' reheating, wrapped in foil, in a medium oven before serving.

MAKES 45–50 APPETISER-SIZED OR 30 LARGE PIROSHKI

PASTRY
—

1¼ cups milk
125 g butter
2 tablespoons sugar
3 cups plain flour
2 teaspoons salt
1 sachet dried yeast
1 egg yolk
beaten egg to glaze

FILLING
—

3 large onions, finely diced
60 g butter
250 g speck or smoked streaky
  bacon, finely diced
freshly ground black pepper

Heat the milk, butter and sugar in a saucepan over low heat, stirring occasionally, until lukewarm and the butter has melted.

Sift the flour with the salt into a large mixing bowl. Stir in the yeast. Make a well in the centre and pour in the milk mixture and egg yolk. Stir with a wooden spoon, gradually incorporating the flour. Beat the dough for 3 minutes, until smooth and elastic. You can use your hands or the dough hook of an electric mixer. Sprinkle a little flour on top, cover with plastic wrap then a folded tea towel, and leave in a warm place until doubled in size, about 1 hour.

Meanwhile, make the filling. Fry the onion in butter in a frying pan over low heat, stirring, until golden, then cool. Add the speck with a good grinding of pepper.

Preheat the oven to 230°C. Turn the dough out onto a floured work surface, knead lightly, and pinch off a tablespoon-sized piece. Flatten it slightly into a thick disc and place a teaspoon of filling on top. Fold the edges over to enclose the filling and mould into a ball. Place on a lightly greased baking tray. Repeat with the remaining dough and filling, cover the baking tray loosely with plastic wrap and leave in a warm place for 15 minutes. Brush with beaten egg and bake for 10–15 minutes, until golden and cooked.

LIGHTLY SALTED DUCK WITH JERUSALEM ARTICHOKE CHIPS

Trine Hahnemann, *Scandinavian Christmas*

We love to cure things in Scandinavia which, of course, comes from a long history of having to preserve food to survive. Now we do it purely for taste and texture. This lightly cured duck also makes a delicious light lunch or starter; simply slice the cooked breasts and toss in a nut oil vinaigrette with salad leaves and walnuts.

SERVES 8

—

3 duck breasts

BRINE

—

4 tablespoons salt
4 tablespoons caster sugar
2 bay leaves
6 cloves
finely grated zest of 1 organic
    orange

ARTICHOKE CHIPS

—

400 g jerusalem artichokes
2 tablespoons olive oil
1 tablespoon salt
freshly ground black pepper

Pour 800 ml water in a large saucepan and add all the ingredients for the brine. Place over medium heat and stir until the salt and sugar have dissolved. Bring the brine to a boil, then turn off the heat and leave until completely cold. Place the duck breasts in a non-reactive dish and pour over the cold brine. Cover with plastic wrap and leave in the refrigerator overnight.

Preheat the oven to 180°C.

Take the duck breasts out of the brine, dry them with paper towel and place in an ovenproof dish. Roast in the oven for 18 minutes; they should remain pink inside.

Wash the Jerusalem artichokes and cut them super-thin (if you have a mandoline, use that). Divide all the slices, keeping them in one layer, between two baking trays lined with baking paper, then drizzle 1 tablespoon of the olive oil over each trayful and sprinkle with salt and pepper. Bake in the oven at the same temperature as the duck for around 25–30 minutes, or until they become crisp and golden. Cool on a wire rack.

Cut the duck breasts into cubes. Pierce a toothpick through the duck and thread the Jerusalem artichoke crisps on top, so each canapé looks like a small sailing boat.

Lars Ranek

INDEX

Published in 2016 by Hardie Grant Books

Hardie Grant Books (Australia)
Ground Floor, Building 1
658 Church Street
Richmond, Victoria 3121
www.hardiegrant.com.au

Hardie Grant Books (UK)
5th & 6th Floors
52–54 Southwark Street
London SE1 1UN
www.hardiegrant.co.uk

A Cataloguing-in-Publication entry is available from the catalogue
of the National Library of Australia at www.nla.gov.au

COOKED: FOOD FOR FRIENDS
ISBN: 978–174379134–9

Publishing director: Jane Willson
Project editor: Ariana Klepac
Cooked editor: Sarah Gamboni
Design manager: Mark Campbell
Designer: Jessica Lowe
Production manager: Todd Rechner

Colour reproduction by Splitting Image Colour Studio

Printed in China by 1010 Printing International Limited